GORDON STRACHAN

GORDON STRACHAN

An Autobiography

with Jack Webster

Stanley Paul
London Melbourne Sydney Auckland Johannesburg

Acknowledgements

Our thanks, for picture and library assistance, are due
to Aberdeen Journals Ltd, the *Scottish Daily Express*,
the *Daily Record* and the *Glasgow Herald*; also to
Alastair Macdonald for statistics and J. Ross Harper
for legal advice.

Stanley Paul & Co. Ltd

An imprint of the Hutchinson Publishing Group

17–21 Conway Street, London WIP 6JD

Hutchinson Publishing Group (Australia) Pty Ltd
PO Box 496, 16–22 Church Street, Hawthorne, Melbourne,
Victoria 3122

Hutchinson Group (NZ) Ltd
32–34 View Road, PO Box 40–086, Glenfield, Auckland 10

Hutchinson Group (SA) Pty Ltd
PO Box 337, Bergvlei 2012, South Africa

First published 1984

Set in Linotron Baskerville by Tradespools Ltd,
Frome, Somerset

Printed and bound in Great Britain by Anchor Brendon Ltd,
Tiptree, Essex

ISBN 0 09 155170 6

Contents

CONTENTS

Introduction

By JACK WEBSTER
author of *The Dons: The History of Aberdeen
Football Club*

In the history of the Dons, published in 1978, I charted
the story of Aberdeen Football Club through its first
seventy-five years, highlighting great occasions and
eulogizing immortal names which had brought colour
and excitement to the Pittodrie story since it began in
1903.

It is part of the fascination of history that it is forever
in the making. As I put the finishing touches to my story
in 1978, how could I have guessed that the best was
lurking round the corner? How could I have known that
a Premier League Championship was about to unfold?
Who would have believed that the European glory of
Gothenburg would explode upon our lives within a few
years?

Into the very tail-end of that Pittodrie story I managed
to make mention of a newcomer, a little red-headed
fellow just signed from Dundee. There was no doubt that
the lad had ability. His skill with a ball gave promise of
things to come but, in 1978, he was still struggling to
establish himself in the Dons' first team.

But if the name of Gordon Strachan was of no
particular significance in 1978, there would be a vastly
different story to tell if the history of the Dons were
rewritten today.

In the years between, the Edinburgh lad with the
Aberdeenshire name has well and truly joined the
immortals. Every generation has its own permutation of

favourites, ranging from Colman, Hume and Hutton, or Jackson, Yorston and Mills to Hamilton, Williams and Baird or Leggat, Buckley and Hather.

A more recent generation will call the claims of Charlie Cooke, Jimmy Smith, Zoltan Varga and Joe Harper, sparking off a lively argument to illustrate once again how wide is the range of public favour.

But whatever the enchantment of distant memory, the Aberdeen team of 1983 will find its own incomparable bracket of immortality. Fifty years from now, youngsters who have mellowed into old age will have every justification for reciting those names of Gothenburg and endowing every one of them with the accolade of heroism.

Wistfully they will remember, like the lingering bouquet of a departed wine, the smooth delicacy of John McMaster. They will regale their grandchildren with tales of Peter Weir's wizardry on the left, which bamboozled the mighty men of Real Madrid. They will tell of Mark McGhee's judicious cross and that flying header from John Hewitt which finally brought the glory of Europe to the bottom of Merkland Road East.

Most of all, I believe, they will be justified in saying that Aberdeen's finest moment coincided with the presence of the two greatest footballers who ever graced the portals of Pittodrie. I speak of Willie Miller and Gordon Strachan – the defender and the playmaker whose combined talents were surely the key which unlocked that gateway to the stars.

In more than forty years of watching the Dons, I have certainly never seen a better player at Pittodrie than Gordon Strachan, the Wee Man with an incredible ability to take on opponents and beat them with the sheer skill of his own twinkling feet.

Yet that talent alone might have done no more than place him in a category of memorable tanner-ba' players who sometimes forgot that there were ten other men in the team.

Allied to individual skill, however, has been his extraordinary vision, a wide-angled appreciation of the entire movement on the field, a shrewd judgement of how best to exploit it and an uncanny accuracy with which to fulfil his purpose. Add to that the knack of scoring goals and the claim that Gordon Strachan may be the greatest Aberdeen player of all time becomes a plausible one.

His part in bringing the League Championship to Aberdeen in 1980 was matched by his emergence as a Scottish international player of world class. With their love of a football artist, the Spaniards acclaimed him as a star of the World Cup Finals of 1982.

Indeed the attention which surrounded him in Spain brought with it the overtures of agents, middlemen and ghostwriters who are never far away when a promising 'property' like Strachan emerges.

The Dons player was bewildered by it all but kept a level head and rejected what may or may not have turned out to be lucrative offers.

As a schoolboy he had shown a rare maturity by rejecting an offer to join Manchester United, with all the glamour that such an opportunity presents. Instead, he accepted the terms of less-fashionable Dundee in the belief that, if he proved his worth at home, he could always take the high road south at a later date. That he was still in Scotland at the age of twenty-seven was the good fortune of Aberdeen Football Club, which he joined in November 1977, during the managership of Billy McNeill.

Though he had turned down the offers of agents, the idea of a book about his illustrious career did, nevertheless, appeal to Gordon Strachan. It was on that memorable night in Munich, when Aberdeen had held the legendary Bayern to a no-scoring draw, that he asked me to collaborate in the writing of it. There are not many people for whom I would have undertaken this task but, as we discussed it over a beer in the lounge bar of the Sheraton Hotel, I knew that Gordon Strachan, one of my own immortal heroes, was certainly one of them.

Football skills apart, I found a touching innocence as well as a thoroughly likeable nature in the man. He and his charming wife Lesley and two tearaway sons, Gavin and Craig, were a welcoming family unit.

Wherever his future may lie, I knew that we had been privileged to live through the greatest era in the history of Aberdeen Football Club and that a major inspiration of that heady period in all our lives had been none other than Gordon Strachan.

His name will live in Pittodrie history long after the personal witness to his talents has disappeared. Whereas most of us today have no clear image of how Benny Yorston or Alec Jackson actually played, those future generations will be able to view the past on a video screen and to judge for themselves the true greatness of Gordon Strachan.

This book is his own memory of the story so far, from his schooldays in Edinburgh to senior football at Dens Park, where he was first-team captain at the age of nineteen, and on to Aberdeen, where he savoured his finest moments.

It is the written record of a man, lively and controversial, who has survived insufferable punishment from an array of uncompromising defenders to enhance the game of football with a level of artistry which it is seldom our privilege to see.

The Wee Man has been magic, all right, carving himself a place in our memories and affections which will grow in significance with the perspective of time.

1

Glory, Glory...

I stood out there in the centre of the Ullevi Stadium trying to convince myself that I wasn't dreaming. Yet who was I to argue with an electronic scoreboard which said that Aberdeen had just won the European Cup Winners' Cup by two goals to one? I had better believe it.

Twelve thousand Aberdonians were already dancing in the dark of those Gothenburg grandstands, apparently convinced it had all happened. Many of them were soaked to the skin but who cared? The players were hugging each other and screaming with delight. Willie Miller was itching to get across to that presentation table to uplift the trophy itself.

Somehow, like Garbo, I just wanted to be alone for a moment. Jumping around has never been my way of celebrating a great occasion and here was the greatest of them all, possibly the highest point in my whole life, and I wanted to stand quietly and take it all in.

Within the next half-hour it would melt away, so I cast my eyes around that stadium, taking in the sight of the jubilant fans enjoying their finest hour in the whole eighty years of the Dons' history.

As a bit of a sentimentalist, I wanted to be able to tell my children and maybe my grandchildren every detail of what happened on the night Aberdeen went to the top of European football.

That achievement was all the greater when we had gained our famous victory over the great Real Madrid, whose white-shirted players were now trooping past me on their way to the dressing room, heads down and hearts even further down. There wasn't a greater club name in the whole world – and we had beaten them! Slowly I began to believe it.

The game had been flashed around the world to millions on television and there wouldn't be many Aberdonians in the furthest corners of the earth who wouldn't already know the great news. The ground beneath us had been churned into a battlefield after the downpour but, as I stood in the mud, I found myself thinking back to the start of the journey in Europe.

Because we were regarded as small fry, it had been necessary to play a preliminary round against Sion of Switzerland. That wasn't too difficult but once we began to face the stiffer opposition, would there be anyone alive brave enough to have forecast that Aberdeen would go all the way to victory in the Cup Winners' Cup? If so, he could have made a fortune at the bookies. Now it had all happened. We had come through those gruelling rounds against Dinamo Tirana of Albania, Lech Poznan of Poland, Bayern Munich of Germany, Waterschei of Belgium and finally the great Real Madrid of Spain.

We had conquered the lot to put the name of Aberdeen Football Club on the map of world soccer as it had never been before. It was sometimes hard enough to convince people that we were at the top end of Scottish football, never mind Europe. But now we were there. And I thought of my greatest fan, my Dad, up there somewhere in the Ullevi grandstand, no doubt waving down to me though I couldn't see him. He had saved to come to Gothenburg and this would be the greatest moment of his life. It was a far cry from our humble home in Edinburgh where I first showed some signs of a talent for football and where he had dreamed dreams that I would be a star one day.

Since then I had played my way through boys' teams to become a professional with Dundee and team captain at Dens Park at the age of nineteen. I had moved on to

Aberdeen in time for the great reign of manager Alec Ferguson, who led us to the Premier League Championship of 1980 and the Scottish Cup win of 1982. It was that victory which paved the way to Europe. I had established myself as a Scottish internationalist, played in the World Cup in Spain and now, to crown it all, here we were champions in Europe.

Back at our hotel there would be celebrations continuing far into that Wednesday night and Thursday morning. And when it was all over I would have time to sit down and take stock of my life so far, a life which had brought me not only excitement but a standard of living very different from what I had known in a decent, working-class home in an Edinburgh housing scheme.

There had been a lot of talk about me leaving Aberdeen but the future could take care of itself. It was time for a nostalgic look at the past and the more I looked at it the more I realized what a tremendous life I have had.

2

Milkboy Days

I was born in Edinburgh on 9 February 1957, and christened Gordon David Strachan, the first child of Jim and Catherine Strachan, ordinary working folk who were staying at the time with my mother's mother in Leith before they got a council house of their own.

As far as I can trace, we have been Edinburgh people for several generations though, with the Gordons having their roots in Aberdeenshire and the Strachans coming from Peterhead, there must surely have been some Northeast blood in me somewhere.

But the background was Edinburgh, where my father worked as a scaffolder at that time and my mother had a job in a whisky bond in Leith. Soon they were to move into a council block at 4/4 Muirhouse Grove, which has been their home ever since. You didn't exactly broadcast to people that you lived in Muirhouse for it was just about Edinburgh's toughest district and has become even more so in recent times with all the modern problems of drugs and so on.

We would rather have said we came from a better district like Silverknowes or Barnton, where I used to deliver milk as a boy, but when your address was Muirhouse Grove you didn't have much chance to put on airs. In any case, there were lots of good folk in Muirhouse, despite the tough elements, and in my case I had an advantage in the fact that the football skills I had begun to develop as a little boy had taken me into competition with older boys who were able to look after me in times of potential trouble.

It was eight years before my sister Laura came along so for a large part of my childhood I was more or less an only child. With my growing interest in football as a boy I didn't see as much of my little sister as I did in later years when she came to visit us in Aberdeen and liked the place so well that she took a job with British Telecom in the city, found herself a boyfriend and settled in as part of the Strachan household in Albury Road.

In those childhood days, however, there were no fancy cars standing outside. It was a working-class home where we tended to live like kings over the weekend, with the menu running a bit downhill during the week until there was soup alone on Thursday and something from the chip shop on Friday. I remember the excitement of looking forward to our holidays and what seemed like the long journeys to Kinghorn and Leven. Looking back on it now, I could actually see some of my holiday spots from my bedroom window in Edinburgh. The big event, however, was the decision to go to Butlin's holiday camp at Ayr and I can still remember the three-and-a-half-hour bus journey to get there. We have pictures in the family album to show the four of us tucking into our dinner at Butlins, with yours truly looking a bit dated in the long-haired styles of the time.

Nearer home I rarely ventured as far as Princes Street and knew nothing about what existed on the other side of it. My little world revolved around Muirhouse where I had become an enthusiastic golfer by the age of eight or nine, playing two or three times a day at Silverknowes Golf Club.

I suppose it is always difficult to pinpoint exactly when you begin to realize that you might have some particular talent and certainly little boys don't start kicking a ball with any thought that they may play for Scotland one day. That can become your dream as you start to grow but you are just pleased to be spending your spare time in playground games with your classroom friends and pretending to be as good as your idols who, in my case, happened to be Pat Stanton and Peter Cormack of Hibs.

At Silverknowes primary school it was class games, in which I played for Mrs Webster's class against Mrs Pemberton's class. With the women knowing nothing about football, Mrs Webster would tell me to pick the team. I had a trial for the school's B team but by the age of nine I was in the first team, with boys two years older than me. If I had had time to stop and think about it I would have realized that I was showing a lot of promise with a ball by that stage. When it came to picking sides after school I was always the first to be chosen and there came a time when they wouldn't allow me to play unless I was in goal. So I started moving up with older boys, where I had a better chance of being allowed to play, and was still turning on the style for the Silverknowes school team, sometimes appearing in Leith school cup finals which used to draw out crowds of more than a thousand people.

The first man to spot that I had something to offer the game was Tom Aitken, the janitor at Groathill School, one of our rival teams, and the man who played a big part in running Edinburgh Thistle, a well-known amateur club.

He was soon to invite me to join Thistle but before then I had moved to the secondary school at Craigroyston, where many of the primary children from the Leith-Granton area came together. It was a tough school, really frightening at times, but once again I had the protection of the older boys who were my team-mates at football.

Craigroyston did well in competitions like the Scottish Junior Shield and I have a newspaper cutting which tells of our fifth round game against Bathgate Academy in which little Strachan 'brilliantly flicked the ball over his left shoulder for the winner.' My father, who has always taken even more joy from my career than I have, was there as usual that night, along with some relations, and when we got back home there were arguments about whether I really planned that winner or whether it was just a fluke.

While football had dominated my life so far, I was actually doing quite well at school, having been sent from the top stream of my year to sit the entrance examination for Trinity School. But my mother and housemaster were becoming concerned about the amount of time I was spending on football.

3

I Become a Hibs Fan

By the age of twelve I was totally immersed in the game, turning out on a Sunday morning with hordes of people, who ranged from my own age up to thirty-five. We played for three or four hours at a time on school ground at the back of our house.

If you had been looking for future stars at that time you might have picked a pal of mine called David McDonald, who was full of all the football tricks but was even smaller than me and ended up playing for Tranent. There were other pals like Ambrose Hunter, John Stupart and Brian Crighton and some good lads from Ferranti, Thistle and Meadowbank.

By the time I was thirteen, Tom Aitken had me playing for Edinburgh Thistle, well out of my age group and, having won everything in the Edinburgh area, we found ourselves in two Scottish Juvenile Under-16 Cup Finals. The first was against St Columba's of Dundee and the opposition included players like Graeme Payne and John Holt, later of Dundee United, and John McPhail of Dundee. We were beaten 5–1.

The other game was even more memorable for there I was, a slip of a lad at fifteen, playing against a Dunfermline team and facing up to a gigantic left back whose gruesome frame was a sight to behold. With everyone talking about his size, he just had to look at me and that was enough to put us on the way to a 2–1 defeat. I never forgot the name of that giant. It was Douglas Rougvie, as big a chunk of muscle at sixteen as he is now.

Tom Aitken and his colleague, Stuart Woollard, were running our Edinburgh Thistle team and playing an important part in my early development. After a game we would all gather back at Tom's house and have a blether about football. I tried to overlook the fact that he was a Hearts supporter, on the grounds that nobody is perfect. By then I was an established follower at the other end of Edinburgh. As early as five I had been taken to see Hibernian and there might have been something prophetic in the fact that the opposition on that very first visit to Easter Road was none other than Aberdeen. The only real memory I have of that occasion was the performance of Charlie Cooke, whose role I was to take over at Pittodrie fifteen years later.

But Hibs became my team from that day onwards. I was too late to see the Famous Five but the lads who were arriving to become heroes of my own day were Pat Stanton and Peter Cormack, Jim O'Rourke, Eric Stevenson, Willie Wilson in goal, Joe Davis, the penalty-kicker, and Bobby Duncan, whom I remember breaking his leg in a tackle with John Hughes of Celtic. We were a noisy lot of youths who used to travel on the No. 16 bus to Easter Road, along by Granton and Newhaven and up Leith Walk, and sometimes the driver would stop the bus and give us a last warning before proceeding to the football ground, where we alighted at Balfour's Bar. With my own playing commitments, however, the visits to Easter Road became more and more confined to Wednesday matches.

By the time I had reached fourteen, in 1971, those commitments had spread beyond the local scene to the Edinburgh Schools Select, where we beat the Glasgow Schools 4–1 in a game at Tynecastle.

It was now inevitable that names of the future were beginning to creep into the team-sheets. Certainly there are always talented schoolboys who are never heard of again but there must be a proportion who will come through. In that inter-city game, the Glasgow team included Alex O'Hara, later of Rangers, and my Edinburgh colleagues included Arthur Albiston, who was to gain prominence with Manchester United and Scotland.

Arthur was also with me when we were chosen to play for Scotland in that under–15 match which now gains so much television attention and produces so many memorable games and top players of the future. Not so long ago it was Paul McStay and Alistair Dick who sprang to prominence in one afternoon at Wembley and were soon to become names with Celtic and Tottenham Hotspur. In 1972, I was in that corresponding team when we held England to a 1–1 draw at Ibrox, and their goal was scored by a small chap called Raymond (Butch) Wilkins. We also played in a much-praised ding-dong game against West Germany at Saarbrucken which ended up at 4–4, in front of a crowd of about 40,000. By then I was getting accustomed to the routine of being fitted out with blazers and boarding aeroplanes for foreign countries, a good preparation for the years ahead of me.

Meanwhile I was growing up in an Edinburgh which was famed around the world for its scenic beauty and international Festival but it was all passing over my head. To this day I have never attended a Festival performance or even seen the Tattoo, which must be a record for an Edinburgh man. I used to wonder why all those foreign visitors were standing there, proudly taking pictures of the castle and it was not until I left the place that I realized Edinburgh was the only city with a castle plonked right in the middle. I had taken it all for granted, in the way you do with familiar things.

My world revolved around football pitches, where I was having a good season with Edinburgh Thistle and approaching that school-leaving age when everything has to be decided about your future. Do you carry on at school and prepare yourself for some kind of job or trust everything to your football talents and a career where there are no examinations, and performance is what decides if you are good enough to make a living or not? Every night my mother was on at me about remaining at school. 'What if you don't make it in football? You have nothing else to fall back on.' It is a natural worry for a parent and maybe my mum was right but my father knew my mind was made up. I had enough confidence in my ability to manipulate a ball to know that, out of my own generation of up-and-coming youngsters, I would surely be among the ones to make the grade in first-class football.

That confidence was bolstered by the fact that a whole string of top clubs were already beating a track to our front door at Muirhouse Grove with offers of trials and contracts to sign. Coventry were first on the scene, followed by Manchester City and I had a note from Tom Aitken to say that Celtic were also coming to watch me play. There was a very courteous and thoughtful letter from Bobby Ancell, a former Aberdeen player who represented Nottingham Forest and wanted me to spend a week down there during the school holidays.

As it happened, I took up none of these offers but when a Mr Dalziel asked if I would like to sign for my beloved Hibs I was jumping with joy at the idea of it. I had to control my delight, however, when we ran into difficulties about the type of form they wanted me to sign. My father, taking his usual interest in my future, was not at all happy about the proposed arrangement.

In the meantime, after his successful run as manager of Aberdeen and winning the Scottish Cup the previous year, Eddie Turnbull had just arrived back at his old club to join up with his longtime friend, Tom Hart, who had gained control and become chairman of Hibs. The new manager thought I was being offered too much of an expenses allowance for boots and so on and he asked to see my father and me. Well, Mr Turnbull was well known for his choice of expressive adjectives and it ended up with him and my father having a bit of a row and my dream of playing for Hibernian Football Club falling apart.

The next man on the scene was Alex Somerville, representing Dundee FC, and that was the start of a story which has baffled many people. With so many opportunities presenting themselves, why should I have landed with a club like Dundee, who had produced a lot of fine players but had failed to make the kind of mark on Scottish football which might have been expected?

4

Old Trafford Offer

In that period of the early 1970s a lot of Scottish boys were heading south to the big English clubs on the same kind of offers as I had. But most of them seemed to return home almost as quickly as they had gone. In my own young mind, I worked out that, if I could make the grade with Dundee, who weren't a bad team in the old First Division of the time, then I could always move south later. If I couldn't make it with Dundee then what was the point? It was an easy train journey from Edinburgh, with several players travelling up and back every day, and that could be my testing ground. But things are not easy for a schoolboy trying to make the best decision at an age when he has no experience of life.

No sooner had I given a verbal undertaking to Dundee than Manchester United were on the doorstep. It so happened that I was out playing football till ten-thirty that night and my Dad took their representative across for a drink at Silverknowes Golf Club until I came home. Imagine the temptation to a young lad being asked to go to Old Trafford, one of the greatest football settings in the world, to begin a career which might have taken me into the top flight of the English game at a very early age. The legendary George Best, they said, would be there to meet me on arrival and the whole prospect seemed like a golden dream to a starry-eyed schoolboy. When I look back on it now, I think it says something for my own personal standards as a boy that I listened to all that temptation and then said firmly, 'No thank you. I have given my word to Dundee and I don't intend to break it.'

I had signed nothing at Dens Park and I doubt if anyone would have blamed me for jumping at the United offer but I did think there was a matter of honour to be considered. Alec Somerville came back to see me, along with the Dundee manager of the day, John Prentice, and his chief scout, Tom Arnott, and I duly signed the forms as planned. That was in 1971, when I was still fourteen, and by the following Easter I was free to leave school and make my way to Dens Park to become a full-time member of the Dundee groundstaff.

John Prentice had made his name as a Rangers player and later became boss of the Scotland team but, in the merry-go-round of football managers, his time at Dundee was to be short-lived and the man who inherited me was Davie White. He had become manager of Rangers when Scot Symon was sacked in 1967 and had more recently been sacked himself. The Dundee coach of the time was none other than Jim McLean, who was soon to move across the street to begin his successful career as manager of United. Personally I was much less concerned about the movement of managers than about my new career as a professional footballer, earning £15 a week and getting up at 6.15 a.m. to catch a bus into Waverley Station and a train over the Forth and Tay Bridges to Dundee. Schoolboys arriving at senior clubs nowadays are inclined to give older players a bit of backchat but I was too scared to open my mouth. I just gazed in awe at names which were well known in Scottish football at that time, people like Doug Houston, Jocky Scott, Gordon Wallace, George Stewart, Davie Johnston, Jimmy Wilson, formerly of Aberdeen, Bobby Wilson and John Duncan, who later went to Spurs.

It is a sign of the changing economic times that Dundee had twelve players travelling from Edinburgh when I was catching that early-morning train. I used to travel up with George Stewart, Bobby Robinson, Bobby Ford and Ian Anderson but, while they could return in the afternoon, I had to continue my groundstaff duties and used to arrive home in a state of collapse about seven o'clock at night. It was too tiring, on top of which I was losing too much money to George Stewart who was the organizer and main beneficiary of the card school. He now owns pubs in Edinburgh and has become a wealthy man but I still tell him that I started him off in business with my mother's allowance!

Three other Dundee players, George Mackie, Davie Johnston and Duncan McLeod, stayed in digs with the mother of Ron Selway, the former Dundee player who had gone to Raith Rovers, and she agreed that I should move in with them. On the first night I managed to break her television set and when I continued to display my aptitude for breaking things, ending up with a precious antique, it was time for me to move away to digs in Broughty Ferry, where I joined up with two more Dens Park men, Alec Caldwell (later of St Johnstone) and Keith Wyllie. The landlady was called Maggie and there was a happy, homely atmosphere about the place, with a constant coming and going of labouring kind of folk. I had some of the best laughs of my life in those digs but we weren't exactly flush with money, to the extent that Bobby Robinson used to give me loans. That attic room wasn't the warmest place in the world but we used to keep a little electric fire burning constantly (and cheaply!) by sticking a match in the meter to gain an illegal supply of power. We discovered that another drain on the electricity supply was caused by Keith Wyllie, who was so tall that he slept with his feet stuck over the end of the bed, with the electric fire positioned to heat them all night!

It was the wild period of my life and since I couldn't stay in that room alone I was inclined to go out on the town with the older lads. It would have been permissible to have a few drinks after the game on a Saturday night but we were out on Tuesdays and Thursdays as well. Alec Caldwell could hold his liquor but after a couple of pints I was gaga and talking a lot of rubbish. We could be found around town in any of those juke-box places and it came to the point where the landlady phoned Davie White to tell him we were going over the score. Even when we were hauled in, like boys to the headmaster's room, it didn't dawn on me that I could easily be out in the dole queue if I didn't watch my step. I was reading too many newspaper reports describing me as a star of the future and believing it was only a matter of time before it all happened. But life doesn't work like that.

Before I learned my lesson, however, I was to become involved in a couple of more serious incidents, one while playing for Scotland's professional youth team in Denmark. After the match I went out on the town with John Holt of Dundee United, Isaac Farrell of Rangers and Rikki Ferguson of Hamilton. It was just a matter of a couple of Carlsbergs but we shouldn't have been there and when Peter Rice, the boss, caught up with us we were banned from the Scottish team. That was not the way to make a good impression at international level nor was it a way to bring credit to your own club. When I arrived home I was scared to mention it to manager White but he found out from the newspapers and I was pulled in and given a real going-over. Although there was still another infamous incident to come, involving the legendary Jimmy Johnstone of Celtic, I was beginning to learn my lesson.

I suppose you can put it down to the process of growing up but, frankly, I would not have been without that daft period in my life.

5

Roasting Alan Ball

Maybe fate was trying to put some good influence my way when I met a girl called Lesley Scott one evening. We arranged to meet again but must have made such an impression on each other that neither of us turned up. Something must have been in the stars, however, because I bumped into her again at a disco five months later and this time we began to get to know each other a little better. With my own shortage of inches, I was always on the lookout for someone who might possibly be smaller and Lesley seemed to fill the bill until I found she was dancing with her shoes off. When she put them back on she was at least as tall as me with my platforms.

But height is not everything and romance began to blossom, as they say in the novels. Lesley was the same age as me and worked with the Cooperative Insurance in Dundee, living with her parents in the grounds of Strathmartin hospital, where her dad was an electrician. By chance, big Alec Caldwell had met his future wife and Keith Wyllie had been given a free transfer by Dundee, which was a fairly lucky break for me since Keith was a boy for the bookies' shops – and still owes me £10 from the betting days!

The outcome of all this was that Alec Caldwell and I moved out of our digs into a rented flat in McGill Street and I was seeing more and more of Lesley. If we went out at night it was invariably to the pictures for we were great film fans and still are. We became engaged at eighteen, by which time I was pushing my way into the

Dundee first team and gaining a fair amount of attention from the newspapers.

But the biggest headline of all came on the Sunday morning after we had played Arsenal in a friendly which marked the laying of a brand new playing surface at Dens Park. My father was there as always and, knowing that I had turned on a rather special performance, he was down at the newsagent's waiting for the papers to arrive before bursting back into our house in Edinburgh with all the kind of reports he had anticipated. The *Sunday Post* headline said: 'STRACHAN ROASTS ALAN BALL – Dundee find a new Billy Bremner.' Writing that Dundee were far more mobile and creative than the high-priced Londoners, Bill McFarlane wrote:

> In eighteen-year-old Gordon Strachan, Dundee undoubtedly had the man of the match. When he was substituted twelve minutes from the end, England skipper Alan Ball led the thunderous standing ovation given to the Edinburgh teenager. Because, for the seventy-eight minutes he played directly against Ball in midfield, Strachan came out well on top and Ball, sportingly, was prepared to admit it. As well as being a good ball player, Strachan has tons of guts and dig in the tackle. A real Billy Bremner in the making, if ever I saw one.

It is flattering for a young lad to read reports like that and, while you have to keep your feet on the ground, it did my morale no harm at all to be compared to the great Billy Bremner and to have outplayed the England captain, Alan Ball, all in one match. Naturally it was my tussles with Ball which gained most people's attention but what nobody seemed to notice was that I was also giving the runaround to an up-and-coming Arsenal player whose name didn't mean much to the Scottish football public at that time. He was Liam Brady, playing alongside such better-known names as Rimmer, Rice, Nelson, Storey, Kidd and one of my own boyhood favourites, Alec Cropley, once of Hibs.

Coming on as a substitute for Dundee that day was a

man who had yet to play an important part in my own career – that remarkable character, Tam Gemmell, who had joined football's elite eight years earlier when he played right back in Jock Stein's famous Celtic team which beat Inter Milan and became the first British side to win the European Cup. Tam was a Lisbon Lion all right and with his golden waves and bubbling sense of humour, it was little wonder they nicknamed him Danny Kaye for he had a strong resemblance to the American film star. Playing into the twilight of his career, he brought a fresh air to Dens Park and had that way with people which made him a natural leader. So Davie White made Tam captain and I found myself playing alongside one of that immortal team which had given such a boost to Scottish football when I was just a boy of ten.

Much to my surprise, when Tam was injured the manager called on me to lead the team so I had the privilege of being captain of Dundee at the tender age of nineteen. Tam regained the captaincy after his injury but he was soon to replace Davie White as manager of Dundee – and he promptly appointed me captain again. In all honesty, however, I was too young for the job. It is a difficult role for which you must have a natural talent and I have never kidded myself that I was a born leader. Oh, I'll chatter plenty in the dressing room and on the field, too, but that doesn't always produce the same results as the strong, quiet man of the dressing room. The perfect example of that is Aberdeen's Willie Miller.

In 1975 Scottish football had reached that point in its evolution when the long-discussed Premier League became a reality and the top ten teams were creamed off to bring a new sharpness to the competition. At the end of that first season our Dundee team was teetering on the brink of being relegated to the First Division (I wish they could sort out some better names for our leagues to avoid the nonsense of going *down* to the First Division!). In fact we missed out on goal difference to both Aberdeen and Dundee United, would you believe? Our local rivals had to draw in their last game of the season, an evening match at Ibrox. There was word that Dundee might go part-time if they were relegated and I couldn't sleep at nights for wondering about my future without full-time football.

My mother's warning about staying on at school began to haunt me and it didn't go away that night as I tuned into the ten o'clock news to hear that Dundee United had, in fact, managed to win the one point they needed. Dundee were down a division but, as it happened, they did not carry out the intended plan of going part-time. Nevertheless, it was not a happy prospect that we faced in the new season at Dens.

6

Jimmy Johnstone and Me

Lesley and I were married in Strathmartin Church, Dundee, in the summer of 1977, when we were both twenty, and moved into a house in Portree Avenue, Broughty Ferry. My team-mate George Mackie was best man and Alec Caldwell was usher. At Dens Park I was heading into a new season of First Division football little knowing that, within three months of the start, I would be on my way to a new club.

Before then, however, Tam Gemmell had decided to enlist the talents of his former Celtic team-mate Jimmy Johnstone, surely one of the greatest ball players the world has ever seen. Johnstone was a legend now at the very end of his career, having been around a few clubs since he left Celtic, but the manager was obviously banking on the fact that genius has always something left to offer, even when it may have come through stormy periods. Jimmy Johnstone had been in and out of trouble even during his great days with Celtic when he would fall foul of Jock Stein. There had also been a much-publicized incident in which he drifted out to sea in a late-night rowing-boat escapade while staying with the Scottish international party at Largs. Tam Gemmell knew he was taking a bit of a chance but by now Johnstone would surely have settled down. To me, there was the prospect of appearing and rubbing shoulders with a true immortal of the football game.

Tam detailed me to go beside Jimmy in training to pull him along at our pace and when I did so I soon discovered that he was shockingly short of fitness. To his credit, however, he really worked hard at pre-season training and when we relaxed he would tell us great stories of the world stars he had met. This was really brushing shoulders with the big-time and I must admit I was a bit awe-struck by the Wee Man.

If I thought he had given up the good life I was soon to be disillusioned, to my own personal cost, in what turned out to be the most notorious incident of my career. It happened one day when Jimmy and I had both been suffering from injuries and it turned into one of those nightmare capers which are not without a touch of comedy when you look back on them later – much later!

While the rest of the lads were away training, Jimmy and I finished our own modified stint at eleven-thirty and he asked if I fancied a bite to eat. I used to be satisfied with a Dundee mince roll at that time of day but Jimmy, who had known a different style of life, conducted me to the Queen's Hotel and ordered a slap-up meal for two, complete with bottle of wine. Well, one bottle turned into two and three and the next I knew I was inviting him home to our place in Portree Avenue, where we continued to drink into the afternoon. Footballers to the last, we suddenly felt like a kickabout with a ball so out we went to the back where we started playing with some local kids. We must have looked a beautiful spectacle! When that was over, we found that we had locked ourselves out of the house and I don't know what the neighbours could have thought of our display as the famous Lisbon Lion tried to hoist the Dundee captain on his shoulders in an attempt to reach the upper window.

We were both such small chaps and in such a state of inebriation that we weren't even reaching the bottom window. Lesley arrived home in the middle of this episode, which might have come from a Keystone Cops farce, and ordered us out, such was the spectacle we were making of ourselves. So we tottered off and Jimmy apparently hailed a taxi and took us somewhere outside

Dundee, where we found ourselves another pub. Even in the depths of a drunken stupor there comes a moment when you know that all is not well. That was the moment when I said, 'Jimmy, I'm totally out of the game. I'll need to go home.'

So we staggered out into the street and were passing a fairly innocent looking building when I found myself looking in at the window – and experiencing something of the horror that Tam o' Shanter must have felt when he looked into the kirk at Alloway. On this occasion, however, Tam wasn't on the outside. His was the face on the inside looking out – the face of our Dundee manager, Tam Gemmell! By a terrible mischance, the village we had reached on our pub crawl was none other than Errol, where big Tam happened to run a hotel. There he was, innocently contemplating the afternoon sunshine when his peace was disturbed by the sight of two of his better-known football heroes, legless as newts, blootered to the eyeballs.

Coming to the door in consternation, he called, 'Where the hell are you two going?'

Pulling myself up to my full height and controlling my tongue slightly better than my legs, I replied, 'Where am I going? I don't even know where I am.'

Big Tam handled the situation with a lot of human understanding, got us organized with transport home, allowed us to sleep it off and wasn't too heavy with the repercussions. But I vowed after that experience that it was never again.

Tam Gemmell was a thoroughly likeable man who knew well what footballers can get up to. He must also go down as one of the few managers who has ever gone visiting one of his players in hospital with a cairry-oot. It happened when I went to Fernbrae Hospital, Dundee, for a final solution to a fungus which had been troubling my toes for some time. The decision was that they would root out my big toenails for ever and, believe me, that can be one of the most painful experiences of your life. With a cage over my feet to protect the delicate tissue when the nail had been removed, I found myself dreaming that I was taking a swipe at the ball. The whole hospital was woken by the noise of my screams in the dead of night as I stubbed my tender toes into that cage.

Tam knew that I would be in need of consoling so he and his assistant, Willie Wallace (another Lisbon Lion), arrived up at the hospital with a bottle of wine and some Export. The manager's gesture was greatly appreciated in the circumstances, believe me.

7

From Dens to Dons

If it comes as a surprise to learn that I play my football without any nails on my big toes, it will come as a bigger surprise to those who praise my great 'vision' to know that I am half-blind in my right eye.

It is a matter which I have kept pretty quiet up until now, but it dates back to my schooldays in Edinburgh when I was walking across the playground one day and someone called on me to join in a kickabout with a ball. I forgot that I was carrying a ballpoint pen in my hand and, as I fell in a tackle, the pen went right into the socket of the eye. It damaged the optic nerve and came within a thousandth of an inch of making me blind. I was rushed to hospital and spent two and a half of the most frightening weeks of my life, with a pad over my eye and the thought that I might never see with it again. It would most certainly destroy any thoughts of top-class football and you can imagine the drama as they finally removed that pad and I found I still had some vision, albeit the half-vision which has stayed with me to this day. It is difficult to describe but the way it affects me is that, if I close my left eye, I can see only the top half of someone I'm looking at. In a vital situation in a goalmouth I will still throw my head at a ball without thought for my safety but there are other times, when a ball may come at me from the right and matters are not so pressing, that I become conscious that further damage could be done to that right eye.

Deprived of toe-nails and proper vision I might have

seemed a proper candidate for the knacker's yard, yet I was still turning on the style for Dundee.

In the light of events to come, it is interesting to find that, in one of those early newspaper interviews where they list a player's favourite food, pop stars, television programmes and so on, I listed my favourite country as Sweden. Little did I know what lay ahead. That choice was made on the basis of a Dundee tour of Scandinavia when Davie White was manager and Tam Gemmell captain. It may even have been coloured by the events of a particular Sunday afternoon when the club officials went off to a reception and the players were left to amuse themselves. Everything in the town was closed. When he called for beer for the boys, big Tam was asked to sign the hotel chit for payment. As we were leaving on the following morning, the players were already seated in the bus when we saw manager White in deep discussion with the boss of the hotel – over a bill for one hundred beers! He stormed on to the bus and said, 'All right. Who the —— is Mickey Mouse?' Needless to say, big Tam confessed to the signature and we were soon on our way with only a temporary strain on relations.

In those Dens Park days Hugh Robertson, the Dundee coach, had taught me a lot about running off the ball and George Stewart had given me a lot of sensible advice for which I shall always be grateful. But by the start of that 1977–8 season I had a feeling that I was getting nowhere and, frankly, I had become bored at Dens Park. Having been there since I was a boy, I was now twenty and in my sixth year with the one club.

Maybe there is something in my nature that I can last only so long in one place because roughly the same number of years had passed at a later stage in my career when I began to feel it was time to leave Aberdeen. But that was all in the future. At Dens Park I did not feel the club was going in the right direction. In fact it was already on the road to the financial debt which was to become public knowledge later on. I had had a lot of time for Davie White as manager and felt he had a lot to offer the game as a tactician. I also had a lot of admiration for the way he handled the strains of a football manager while at the same time coping with the worry of his wife becoming a permanent invalid.

In contrast to White's quieter, steady ways, Big Tam Gemmell was, as I have indicated, a totally extrovert character, a cheerful bloke who was glad to be one of the boys and to spread a little happiness wherever he went. But as one of the Lisbon Lions, Tam had achieved everything possible in the career of a Scottish footballer and my experience of managers is that the best of them are usually the ones who have not sampled the heights of success as players. Their careers as managers become an attempt to make up for all the things they feel they have missed. Tam's career as a player was more illustrious than that of Alec Ferguson but Fergie's hunger for success is now far greater. In contrast to the efforts of Fergie, Tam would be off home by two o'clock. And there was one occasion when he was late for the team bus. Fergie, on the other hand, is there all the time, setting the standard. If anything, that total dedication was even more apparent in his former assistant Archie Knox, who didn't achieve much as a player but sat in that dugout as if his whole life depended on what was happening out on that field.

The fact that Fergie and Archie would argue and shout at each other during a match was only an indication of their commitment to achieving the very best in football.

Managers apart, I became aware that the spirit had gone out of the Dundee players. They had no feeling for the club and were simply going through the motions. Though I had no thoughts of where I wanted to go, I was anxious to get away before I was caught up in this couldn't-care-less attitude. I asked for a transfer and was slightly surprised that Tam agreed to it so readily. With my size, he apparently didn't think I was making the grade in matters like handling myself in all the kicking and shoving that went on. There was talk of a swop with

Brian McLaughlin of Celtic but it was only a rumour and nothing happened until Tam called me in one day and asked if I would like to go to a Premier League club. That was what sent us on a journey to Aberdeen that same day for what was intended to be an exchange deal involving Jim Shirra and Jocky Scott going to Dundee and me going to Pittodrie. I was excited about what lay ahead. Billy Pirie, who had been with the Dons, spoke a lot about Aberdeen and everyone seemed to agree it was a lovely city to live in. But the whole deal ran into an immediate snag when Jocky Scott, who had been with Dundee before, said he wasn't satisfied with his part of the exchange. I went for a meal with the Aberdeen manager of the time, Billy McNeill, while Jocky went off to think about it. Afterwards there was no agreement and my spirits dropped.

For the moment at least it was all off though Billy McNeill did say as we left to return to Dundee that he hoped something could still be worked out. In fact it didn't take long. The very next morning Tam Gemmell called me to say it was all on again. This time Billy McNeill came to Dundee with an offer involving only Jim Shirra and myself, plus a cash balance payable to Aberdeen of around £50,000. Everybody seemed satisfied. Jim Shirra, who had gone to Aberdeen from Falkirk as one of Ally MacLeod's signings, was the kind of player Tam Gemmell was looking for and the Dundee boss underlined the fact by naming him as captain of his new team for the following Saturday.

As Billy McNeill completed the signing he was quoted as saying:

> This may not be the biggest signing Aberdeen have ever made but, in my opinion, it could well become the best. After all, Gordon is only twenty and the club can expect at least another ten years from him. It's a great signing for the future and I'm sure the Pittodrie fans will come to realize his great ability.

It is not for me to say how accurate was the forecast of

Billy McNeill. All I know is that I was delighted to be moving on to a club which was showing such ambition. Pittodrie was not exactly unknown to me, of course. Though they may not have remembered that I was playing that night, not many Aberdeen fans would have forgotten the last occasion I appeared for Dundee against the Dons. It was on that dramatic night of Wednesday 2 March 1977, when the poor relations from Dens Park came north for the replay of a Scottish Cup tie, having drawn on the previous Saturday, and shocked the football world by knocking the Dons right out of the Cup.

As we drank champagne and celebrated those two great goals by Bobby Hutchinson, who had been playing junior football in Aberdeen not so long before, little did we know that an even bigger shock was brewing up behind the scenes. For that was the night an anonymous caller phoned the offices of *The Press and Journal* and claimed that he had evidence of three Aberdeen players laying bets of £500 each at odds of 8–1 in favour of a Dundee victory. The whole thing blew up into front-page news but when the Grampian police completed their investigations, they came up with the conclusion that could have been predicted all along – that the whole thing was a load of rubbish.

Now I was switching my allegiance to Pittodrie and the last thing on my mind was money. For the record, I was stepping up from £75 a week to £85 a week, but what I did fail to realize was that I had agreed to a signing-on fee which was too low. I was giving up a semi-detached house in Dundee which would fetch £10,500 and was going to have to buy a comparable one in Aberdeen for £14,500. I went back to discuss it with the club and they came up with the extra money to buy the house. But fixing on a house takes time, especially when you are thrown immediately into the football arena to be judged by fans who may never have been aware of you before and want to see if you were worth buying in the first place. A move like that can be a bit diverting so I spent my first five months in Aberdeen staying at the Ashley

House Hotel, at the foot of King's Gate, which had also been the temporary resting place of both Billy McNeill and Ally Macleod when they arrived as new managers at Pittodrie. Just married that year, Lesley stayed on at her work in Dundee for the first two months and I settled in at the Ashley with Charlie and Ruth Rettie, who were the ideal kind of people to be looking after you at a time which was bound to be unsettling. Of course I wasn't alone. In his short term as the Dons' boss, Billy McNeill had not exactly been idle in signing new players. Having come to Aberdeen from Clyde, he was not long in bringing the Shawfield star of the day, Steve Archibald, to join him in Aberdeen for a very modest fee. Beavering away at improving his squad, he remembered another promising lad who had disappeared to England and was now with Notts County. He soon unearthed him and introduced the name of Ian Scanlon to the Pittodrie terracings. To complete his signings, he brought Steve Ritchie from Hereford and all four of us were billeted with Charlie Rettie, meeting up in the kitchen late at night to make tea and take part in great discussions about football. Steve Archibald had just turned full-time footballer, having been a motor mechanic in Glasgow, and Ian Scanlon was quickly proving to us all that, if he had not been a brilliant ball player, he could easily have made a living as a comedian. There was never a dull moment when the Scan was around, as any of his team-mates will tell you. Of course the story got around that he was also a budding millionaire. Despite the obscurity of Notts County, he had gained himself publicity before coming to Aberdeen when the newspapers told a great story of his prospects of wealth. In an interview, he had apparently given the impression that he wouldn't be depending on football for too long because of all the money that would be coming from his girlfriend's aunt. What wasn't so obvious at first was that, whatever she intended doing with her money, the aunt was as fit as a fiddle and in no hurry to leave this earthly scene!

I plucked up courage to raise the subject with him one

night and it became a bit of a joke after that. With all his dreams of big cars and foreign travel, he always intended to sample life in America. When he eventually went to St Mirren I remember asking him about it and he replied that by leaving Aberdeen for Paisley, he was at least moving down the road towards Prestwick Airport! Billy McNeill put an insurance broker at my disposal to advise about the money to spend on a house and where to look, and we finally moved into 187 Jesmond Avenue in the Bridge of Don district, out past the Baker Oil Tools premises. It later became quite a popular area with Dons players. Just as others had clustered around Westhills, Jim Leighton, Doug Bell and Peter Weir moved out to the same district as Lesley and I had chosen in those early days in Aberdeen.

Before I had time to think about houses, however, I found myself in the Aberdeen team on that very first Saturday, which was Guy Fawkes Day 1977, playing Dundee United at Tannadice where we won by the last-minute goal from one of football's characters, Ian Fleming. The midfield that day was Joe Smith, Davie Robb and myself. I now had time to look around my adopted city and felt that I was going to be really happy there.

8

McNeill's Misery

If I thought I was going to be happy in Aberdeen as a city, any idea of finding immediate joy on the football field was short-lived. On my first Monday at Pittodrie we had a training session and I went to tackle a young trialist from Nairn. In doing so I went over on my ankle and was in hospital within half an hour for a checkup. In my desperation to make my home debut against Ayr on the Saturday I was receiving injections. I made the team that day but not with any distinction, though I managed to score in the next game, against Motherwell, when Davie Robb had a hat trick.

I was still struggling with that first injury when we met St Mirren and their stocky full back, Alec Beckett, came at me with one of those tackles which put me out of the game for the next four weeks. I don't know what his manager, Alec Ferguson, thought of it but to me it was one of those rash, silly tackles which football could well do without. It damaged the ligaments of my ankle and that was me out of the Aberdeen team before I had had time to play a decent game. My place in the team was taken by John McMaster, who grasped at his chance and was brilliant from then until the end of that 1977–8 season. When I recovered from that injury I was playing in the reserves, managing to regain a first-team place only in cup games because Steve Archibald was already cup-tied with Clyde. I would come in on the right wing for the one game and then, when the League resumed, I was back as a substitute or travelling with Teddy Scott and his reserves.

In this highly unsatisfactory start to my Aberdeen career you can imagine how disappointed I was that I had not been able to show that Billy McNeill had not made a mistake in signing me from Dundee. With the dismal beginning, it even occurred to me that they may want to get rid of me. I felt on edge and was desperate for the chance to play a few good games to show what I could really do.

Being at such a low ebb, I wasn't helped by the unbelievable amount of stick I was taking from the fans. Newcomers usually get a honeymoon period in which to settle but they were cutting mine to the minimum. Mind you, I couldn't blame them for giving vent to their disappointment. If I had gone along to see the kind of rubbish I was playing I would no doubt have felt the same way. Yet, without being bigheaded, I knew I was a good footballer and that it must be only a matter of time before things began to come right for me. However long that was going to take, it was still showing no signs of happening towards the end of the season when I found myself in the Dons squad to meet Partick Thistle. Having started the game on the bench, I remember glancing through the partition between the two dugouts and seeing manager Bertie Auld performing his usual histrionics, complete with that ridiculously large cigar. Sitting beside him was another familiar face, in fact a very good friend of mine, George Mackie, who had not only been my team-mate at Dundee before moving to Firhill but was also best man at my wedding a few months earlier. Like myself, George was a substitute that night but I took the field before he did and proceeded to play just as badly as I had been doing for most of that dismal season.

It was an end-of-season encounter and when George eventually came on he passed by, obviously full of sympathy for my plight, and tried to cheer up an old pal by saying, 'It's OK, Wee Man, I've come on to help you out. Just run up to me and I'll fall down!' The joke, if you could see the funny side of it, was that the first time I ran up to George I fell down before he could! That is how bad I was.

We had a practice game next day and the form of the previous night continued. Billy McNeill had obviously had enough. I saw him coming towards me with finger pointing, ready to give me a dressing down. He said he had been brave enough to put his head on the chopping block for me and what was I doing in return? Just causing him problems and frustration. McNeill had brought his old team-mate from Celtic Park, John Clark, to be his assistant at Pittodrie and I learned later that, if Clark had had anything to do with it, I would never have been signed for Aberdeen. Apparently he didn't fancy me as a player at that stage. The only consolation of those days was being in a reserve team looked after by such a marvellous man as Teddy Scott, one of the great unsung heroes of football. Quiet and thoughtful and ready to encourage, Teddy is the all-Aberdeen man who has spent his life with the club, feels deeply about it and represents the continuity which is necessary when players and even managers come and go through the years. The team-lists would go up on the board after training on Friday and you would be waiting to see who was playing where. But Ted would drop you a hint at training, saying things like, 'I'll make you captain tomorrow.' He has a fine sense of humour and a sensible way of handling people.

My problems at that time were not all on the field, as I have said. Lesley and I were living in a hotel, getting used to married life in a situation where you couldn't even have a decent row because there would always be another ten people sitting around the lounge. We were just twenty, the pair of us, and it takes time to adjust from being a boy to a married man with a wife to look after. It takes time even to get used to somebody sleeping beside you when you have been accustomed to a whole bed to yourself. On top of that was the demoralizing business of looking for a house, putting in bids, waiting for the result and finding that you were nowhere near the final price. Finally we got ourselves settled in that house at the Bridge of Don, complete with our big white dog Olly, who became the centrepiece of the household.

The football in my first season at Pittodrie petered out in that miserable Scottish Cup Final in which Aberdeen were beaten 2–1 by Rangers at Hampden Park, the day Steve Ritchie scored that consolation goal for the Dons from just under the Rangers crossbar, a crazy kind of goal in which I don't think Steve had a clue about where the ball was going. I remember Billy McNeill standing out there in the pre-match line-up of players and managers, facing Rangers at Hampden for the first time without being a Celtic player. He must have had a few private memories coming back to him at that moment but any thoughts of glory were not going to be repeated on that particular day. As fourteenth man, I was sitting on the bench fully clothed, without any prospect of being on the field. Rangers carried off the cup, as had been their habit, and the Aberdeen party returned to the Station Hotel in Perth where there was some kind of reception.

Frankly I wasn't in the mood for any kind of reception and went off to bed very early. The only bright spot of that weekend came on the following afternoon when we drove back to Aberdeen and were treated to a welcome home from a large crowd of fans inside Pittodrie. It drove home the point of how loyal people can be and the lads felt pretty badly that they had not been able to give them something to cheer about. Billy McNeill made a very moving speech through the loudspeaker and promised better things to come. When you look back on it you realize just how far and how fast things have moved at Pittodrie since that Sunday in 1978. Even to appear in a Scottish Cup Final was apparently cause for celebration just those few years ago. In the period since then, nothing short of victory is worth a cheer. When I come to tell you what went on behind the scenes after the Scottish Cup Final of 1983 you will realize just how much the situation has really changed!

In 1978 we went home with a feeling of sadness for the fans and, in my own case, a sense of relief that the season was over. Rangers had dominated once more, winning the treble, and seemed to be on one of their spells of ascendancy. But, as so often happens when things seem to be going well, there were surprises round the corner. Despite his success as manager at Ibrox, Jock Wallace shook the football world by immediately announcing his resignation. Without explanation or any other job in mind he was just walking out of a job which would have been regarded at that time as the best in Scotland. All kinds of rumours circulated as to why he left so suddenly but to this day Wallace has kept his silence.

Even he could not have foreseen the repercussions which would follow. Rangers took the bold step of promoting their popular captain, John Greig, to the manager's chair and that was only the beginning. The great days of Celtic supremacy had come to an end and their board obviously thought they should match the move of Rangers and appoint someone from Greig's generation. The obvious candidate was Billy McNeill, their own true Celt who had led them up the stairway to receive the European Cup in 1967, the first British footballer ever to do so. His master and mentor, the great Jock Stein, was now stepping aside and it was only a matter of days before McNeill was announced as the new manager at Parkhead, after just one year at Pittodrie. John Clark went with him as assistant and it was a strange sight to see the pair of them, returning almost immediately for a Celtic fixture at Pittodrie, getting all heated up in the dugout in opposition to the team which had been their own responsibility just a week or so before.

The reaction of the Aberdeen players to McNeill's departure was fairly predictable. Those who had become regulars in the team were a bit low because they felt that, at last, they were going somewhere. It is always the same with a change of manager. Those in possession wonder if their positions will be threatened. Will the new man like them? Will he want to make his mark by showing that he doesn't depend on a predecessor's choice? A player like John McMaster, who had taken my place and performed so well, must have been wondering what was going to happen to him. Those on the fringes were the ones with the greatest feeling of hope.

9

This Man Fergie

I had a very high regard for Billy McNeill as a manager but, frankly, his departure from Pittodrie came as a great relief to me. Knowing how I had let him down, it was like a burden lifted from my shoulders when I didn't have to face him any more. Psychologically it was a lucky break for me.

The guessing game about who would succeed McNeill didn't have to last too long. In the week of all this activity, as if there had not been enough to talk about concerning Scottish managers, St Mirren sacked Alec Ferguson. There was talk of rows between him and the board which seemed a great pity when he had built the best team anyone could remember at Love Street. He had unearthed players like Frank McGarvey, Tony Fitzpatrick, Peter Weir and Billy Stark (and an unknown called Dougie Bell) and kept them happy for years when they might have been off to England, where McGarvey and Fitzpatrick later went. Though Fergie seemed a likely candidate for Pittodrie, some people wondered if the bad publicity surrounding his departure would put the Aberdeen directors off the idea. To their credit, they had confidence that the former Rangers player was the man to lead them to better times. The timing of his sacking at Love Street had been perfect!

So with everyone wondering what the new boss would mean to us, we awaited the start of that new season, 1978–9. He came fairly quietly among us at first, maybe a bit wary of the fact that he wasn't much older than some of the senior players. As he worked his way into the job, it seemed at times as if some of our older lads were trying to run the training sessions, dictating how free kicks should be taken and so on. He listened and took it all in. Maybe he listened too much at first. But there came a time when he seemed to say to himself, 'Enough is enough.' It was time to start doing things his way. His confidence was growing and he was bringing the players round to his way of thinking, which has since proved to be the right way, at least for ninety-eight per cent of the time. He may have thought at first that players like Bobby Clark and Joe Harper knew more about the game than he did but he was soon to prove that nobody in Britain knew more than him. In the years between then and now I am in no doubt that, whatever I may have thought of him at times, Alec Ferguson has shown himself to be the greatest tactician in the game today.

Of course he had his own bit of sorting out to do. There were players who had to go. Everyone got a chance but if there was any doubt about their total dedication to what they were doing then they were not the people for Fergie. The kind of people I am thinking about included a player for whom I had the greatest admiration – Joe Smith.

He suffered from comparison with his more famous brother Jimmy, who went from Aberdeen to Newcastle and was soon out of the game with a bad injury. So he was greatly underestimated by many people. For Joe had a really great football brain and was a tremendous passer of a ball. Personally, I rated him as a player of the highest potential. But he didn't work hard enough at his game or give enough of himself. So that kind of player was soon on his way and within six or seven months Fergie had everything moving in his direction. He was working to a pattern of behaviour we would all come to know so well, adopting the style which suits him best – screaming at players and putting the fear of death in them!

As far as tactics were concerned, he didn't try to pin

me down to every detail of my game, believing that individual talent must have some expression within the framework of the team. But he gave us a basic pattern to work to. One of the most important gifts in football is to spot what is going wrong on the field. If you don't see that, you can't change it. Therein lies one of Alec Ferguson's greatest assets, the reason he can so often change the pattern of a game at half-time and set us on the road to victory. Jock Stein built a reputation for that same talent in his great days with Celtic. I count myself as being fairly well aware of what is going on during a game and reasonably quick to spot when things are not working out according to plan. But it will still take a player like me half an hour to see where the flaw lies and decide how it could be put right. The difference with Alec Ferguson is that he can do it all in ten minutes.

When he puts it to you at half-time, you realize the remedy was staring you in the face and you wonder why you didn't tumble to it. He shapes and moulds us into a team, allowing just enough of our individual talents to heighten the performance of the team. There are times, for example, when big Doug Rougvie gets carried away with his own undoubted skills and something which may be delighting the crowd suddenly lands the team in trouble. So big Doug gets the message to keep it simple and when he does that he can be a tremendous performer, as he proved on our greatest of all nights.

Many people ask me what this man Ferguson is really like and I find him very hard to explain in a way that people would understand. For a start, although I shall call him Fergie for the benefit of the fans who read this book, the players never call him anything but 'The Boss'. As I say, he puts the fear of death in people. Mark McGhee has known the force of a snooker ball when things went wrong. Fergie's half-time crackups have really to be seen to be believed. Put together, they could be made into a best-selling video programme. They work with most players but not all of them, depending on their temperament. Those half-time storms upset players like

Walker McCall, but they work well with Doug Rougvie, that big, open-faced Fifer who is such a favourite with the crowd. I have seen Fergie screaming at big Doug, facing up to him in the dressing room and stabbing a finger at him. Then later, when there is time to look back on it, he has turned to me and said, 'You know, the big man could have picked me up and used me for toilet paper. He's going to hit me one day.'

Fergie hates being beaten by his old club, St Mirren, and there was one day at Love Street when he kicked a plate of sandwiches up in the air. A ham sandwich came tumbling down on me. A cheese one landed on John McMaster. It's a pity he didn't manage to target one on Neil Simpson for, even with all that mayhem in the dressing room, Neil would just calmly have eaten it, such is his appetite for food.

On another occasion, when we met Arges Pitesti in a European game, we had been playing to a new-fangled system of five men in midfield, with me playing a kind of wide-wide-right role and not getting to grips with it very well. From the bench, Fergie was shouting and bawling at me and things were getting no better as a result of it. So, in a rash moment, I turned and shouted back, 'Away and shut your face!' That did it. I heard no more of him till half-time but I knew that that was a bad sign. I would hear plenty then. As soon as we reached the dressing room I could see him making a beeline for me. There was trouble in store. What happened next could have looked like comedy to a bystander but laughter was totally out of order in my position. As he swung one hand away to the left, he swept a row of teacups in the direction of Willie Miller and Alec McLeish. As he swung the other hand in my direction he upset the tea urn which landed on the floor – and he hurt his hand in the process! It had all arisen because we had thrown away the advantage we had built up and the day for me was saved in the end only by the fact that I scored the penalty goal which took us through.

Nobody escapes the wrath of Fergie. So there are two

ways to look at his behaviour: you can either go in a huff, in which case you won't be around Pittodrie for too long, or you can grit your teeth and say to yourself, 'I'll show that sod!' The second way is, of course, exactly what he wants so he is not a bad psychologist. If he has eleven men out there determined to show him a thing or two then the chances are that Aberdeen Football Club is getting the best out of its players. You can criticize him for his style of handling players but it seems to be the only way he works effectively and he can always turn round and show you his record as a football manager. Not many men in the game have achieved even a fraction of Fergie's success so there you have the answer.

In view of all I have just said about him, you might think that my relations with him are not the best. In fact, I not only have the greatest respect for the man but I actually like him as well! I certainly bless the day when he was chosen as Aberdeen's manager because it was possibly the best thing that has ever happened to my career. I wouldn't have reached international level without him. He is prepared to give everyone a fair chance, but at the same time he keeps you on your toes. When I discovered at the end of his first season that he was trying to sign Billy Stark of St Mirren (four years before he finally succeeded) I knew there was no room for complacency on my part. At the same time he gave me faith in myself, so badly needed after those early days at Pittodrie. When he wasn't shouting at us there was a fine flow of Glasgow patter, which I enjoyed.

Life began to get even better when he had the good sense to appoint my old hero Pat Stanton as his assistant. Apart from the fact that it brought me into contact with the player I had idolized most of all in my early days as a Hibs fan, Pat was the only other person at Pittodrie who came from Edinburgh. If the others were not from Aberdeen they were from the West of Scotland and it was good to have someone who could talk to me about Leith Walk and who knew where the Playhouse was. It made me feel at home. Pat was also good with the quiet word, coming round in the aftermath of Fergie's furies to explain what he had been trying to say and making us all feel human again.

In that 1978–9 season I was sampling my first venture into the European Cup Winners' Cup, little knowing what fate had in store for us in that same competition a few years later. My memory of that contest concerns Bulgaria, where we played Marek Dimitrov and found ourselves with a three-hour bus journey from Sofia and living in a town where there were pigs wandering about the streets and people walking around like zombies, all appearing, disappearing and reappearing in one mass. Where they were going to or where they had come from I never found out but I'm told this is common in Communist countries, in which they all come from the factories together, head for the shops together and presumably vanish to their suburban blocks together like people in regiments. Without going into the politics, it looked a pretty dismal way of life, not improved by their television service which was once again about nothing but factories, workers and people cleaning out pigsties.

The toilet arrangements in the hotel were primitive and I had difficulty in getting to sleep in the place. I was sharing a room with big Willie Garner, who had been telling me that he had just bought a dog. I finally managed to drop off to sleep, although not very peacefully, and the next thing I remember is half-waking to hear big Willie's voice saying, 'Nice doggy, lovely doggy, daddy will take you for a walk!' I jumped up trying to fathom out this crazy nightmare when I saw Willie sitting at the end of his bed, patting his Adidas bag and telling it he would take it for a walk! I got him back to bed and he couldn't remember a thing about it next morning.

Within the next twenty-four hours poor Willie wouldn't have been able to take himself for a walk, never mind his dog or the travelling bag. For that was the night he broke his leg. Imagine choosing Bulgaria as the country to have your leg broken. He was taken to

hospital, a real ramshackle place which didn't give him
much confidence in the staff's ability to put the bones
right. Evidently they used the same theatre for everything and big Willie was lying on a stretcher outside,
waiting for his plaster-cast. He was in enough misery as
it was but from his vantage point he could see right into
the theatre – with the view of a girl having her leg
amputated! They say nature has a habit of putting you to
sleep at moments like that and he was just glad to end up
with both legs intact when they returned him to our
room that night.

A Dons fan who had found his way to this depressing
country landed up on our bedroom floor that night so
there I was with a stranger asleep on the floor and big
Willie screaming in agony as some bandaging became
too tight for him.

There are all kinds of hazards in a footballer's foreign
travel but you get accustomed to it in time and you try to
reassure the younger players who haven't been through
it all before. The Romanians, for example, like to take
you on long, roundabout bus journeys to try and put you
off your game. When it came to a country like Bulgaria I
just said to some of the youngsters, 'It could be worse,
lads. You could live here.'

In that same season we reached the final of the
Scottish League Cup. In fact we reached it twice in the
same year, 1979, because of a change in the system. On
that first occasion we met Rangers at Hampden, a match
which is perhaps best forgotten as the one when Doug
Rougvie, playing his first ever match at the national
stadium, was sent off in the much-publicized incident
with Derek Johnstone. Doug says he was baited – and
that, in the end, he was sent off for absolutely nothing.
Johnstone had gone down in an incident which brought
roars from the Rangers crowd, in the way that these
people can manage to exaggerate the smallest matter if it
might work to their advantage.

I don't think the referee saw anything and big Doug
maintains his innocence to this day. I have known

occasions, years later and over a few beers, when a player has admitted that maybe he wasn't as innocent as he claimed at the time. But five years later and no matter how many beers he consumes, Doug is still adamant that he didn't even touch Johnstone let alone foul him.

Whatever the truth of it, the big man was in a flood of tears and quite inconsolable that day. Players carry the main responsibility for what happens inside a football ground and all I can say is that the Derek Johnstone incident created a bitterness which has affected Aberdeen–Rangers games ever since. As for the match itself, we played well for an hour and were a goal ahead. Bobby Clark had to leave the park with an injured arm and Rangers equalized. With big Doug ordered off and the defence in a bit of disarray, it looked as if the world was against us. Steve Archibald had been told to cover Colin Jackson at corners but the big man got away from him and had a free header at goal. The fact that I played well was little consolation for a day which will be remembered by us all as a sickener.

On the lighter side, a newspaper interviewed me at the time on my likes and dislikes and so on and this was how it turned out:

Favourite players: Tony Fitzpatrick and Ian Scanlon
Favourite 'other team': the Welsh rugby side
My international honours: capped for schoolboys, professional youth and under-21s
Influence in my career: Hugh Robertson, Dundee coach
Biggest drag in football: size of the park
If not a footballer, what would you like to be? A photographer for *Mayfair*.
Would like to meet: John Cleese
Main likes: cinema, golf
Main dislikes: Ian Fleming's elbows; my dog barking at night
Favourite meal: Steak and chips
Best country visited: Sweden (that in 1978)
Favourite TV programmes: *Fawlty Towers* and the *News*
Favourite singers: Frank Sinatra, Dean Martin, Elvis Presley

Favourite actor and actress: Clint Eastwood, Miss Piggy
Favourite holiday resort: Carstairs!
Best friends: My wife, Alec Caldwell

On reflection, Tony Fitzpatrick and Ian Scanlon would now have to make way for Falcao of Brazil as my favourite footballer, in the light of my World Cup experience.

Around the time of that dreadful Cup Final with Rangers there was the consolation of learning that Lesley was expecting our first child, due towards the end of that year. If we had known the kind of energy Gavin was to show later, we might have guessed he would turn up a bit early. We were due to play Hearts on the Saturday and I had left Lesley doing her shopping and going for a walk on the Friday. The Aberdeen party had travelled to my native city and we were staying at the Post House, not far from the Zoo at Corstorphine. Being animal daft, it was a fair bet I could be found there on Saturday morning. I remember I was throwing divots at the polar bears in the water when some of our lads appeared as if they intended to throw me to the bears. Instead they were bringing the news that a neighbour had had to rush Lesley to Fonthill maternity hospital and that she had just produced a son. My first boy! It gives you a strange feeling of confidence and buoyancy, so much so that I went through the game that afternoon at Tynecastle not even flinching when Drew Busby came at me with boots flying and elbows working overtime.

The buoyant feeling took a bit of a dip that same month when we met Dundee United in our second League Cup Final of 1979. We had beaten Rangers and Celtic on the way to the final. On the big day at Hampden we had played well enough to win, a verdict which should have come with a Willie Garner ball which stuck in the mud right on the goal-line. If that didn't do it then surely it would come when Stevie Murray, the former Aberdeen captain who was then turning out for United, shoved Drew Jarvie in the back. I was so convinced it was a penalty that I was already collecting the ball and working out in my mind's eye exactly where I was going to place it in the net. To my consternation we didn't get the award, the score remained blank and we were on our way to a replay at Dens Park, Dundee, the following week. That will surely remain in everyone's memory as the most atrocious weather in which they have ever seen a football match played.

Because of our superiority at Hampden everyone thought it was a foregone conclusion that we would win the replay. The rain was teeming down as we headed south on the day of the match, stopping at Arbroath for a sleep in the afternoon. There was something unreal about the whole occasion. Among the fans heading for Dens that night were Steve Archibald's parents, driving up from Glasgow. In hurricane conditions, their windscreen was shattered and it took a passing motorist – Bobby Clark's brother George – to stop and get Mrs Archibald to the match on time. Her husband arrived later. To their credit, United adapted to the quagmire conditions much better than we did, playing longer passes while we tried the shorter ones. They won 3–0 and we ended up at a reception back in Arbroath with Mr Donald, the chairman, trying to cheer us up with a plate of stovies. It was hard to believe we had been involved in a real game that night.

10

That Day at Easter Road

Before that bleak winter experience, however, Aberdeen
had embarked on a league season which was to prove a
turning point for us all. Who would have imagined when
we started out in August 1979, that so much would be
opening out for us by May 1980? The Aberdeen board
had been talking about working to a long-term plan but
the best laid schemes don't always come off in a
competitive game like football and it is to the credit of the
directors that they were seeing so far ahead and moving
towards their target.

We may have lost two League Cup Finals in one year
but things were beginning to take shape. It didn't look
too promising when we drew 1–1 with Eintracht Frankfurt in the UEFA Cup first-leg match at Pittodrie. But in
the return game we put up an absolutely fantastic
performance and, although we went out of the competition on a single-goal decision in Germany, we started
attracting a lot of attention on the continent. At the end
of the Frankfurt match the Germans gave us a standing
ovation and their manager Friedal Rausch said afterwards:

My team is within one point of the top of the Bundesliga
and we beat Hamburg – Kevin Keegan and all – last
week but they did not give us as many problems as
Aberdeen. I was really impressed, particularly in the first
half when they could have scored twice. We had to work
really hard for this victory. Keeper Bobby Clark and
Gordon Strachan were the top players. In defeat, Aber-

deen were gentlemen and did not resort to tough play. We have found friends in this team.'

Alec Ferguson said we could have sealed the tie in the first half when we had them on their knees but were unable to produce the killer punch. He added, 'But this has been a good European experience. Eintracht are top class and my players will have learned a lot from this game.'

Even the Spanish referee was so impressed that he joined in with these comments, 'Both teams played as true professionals. There were no men posing injuries or play-acting. Aberdeen got on with the game and showed a high degree of skill. I am convinced they will soon become a big name in European soccer.'

How is that last sentence for a piece of forecasting? His fellow-countrymen of Real Madrid should have been listening! It is interesting that they thought we might have resorted to tough tactics, as if that was the expected thing. But it is not our style and we have made many friends on the Continent because of it. Another lesson to come out of that game was that, if you look after yourself, you can last for a long time. Two of the Eintracht players were well through their thirties and in such perfect condition that I became all the more convinced we pack in too soon in this country. I certainly intend to be around well into my thirties.

All that was taking place in October 1979, but even by spring of the following year it looked as if Celtic were going to walk away with the Premier League. Our very last chance of giving ourselves any hope at all came in a midweek game at Celtic Park when a victory for the Parkhead side would practically assure them of the championship. That very fact put the pressure on the home side and the Aberdeen players were remarkably relaxed. I can remember a lot of hilarity in the dressing room and Bobby Clark coming in rather seriously and saying, 'I hope you lads are laughing tomorrow.'

Well, we were laughing all right. Steve Archibald, Mark McGhee and myself scored in a 3–1 victory and at that late stage in the season the championship was still a possibility for Aberdeen. I had missed a penalty that evening and was taking the usual amount of stick from the Celtic fans. So victory was all the sweeter when I scored my goal and ran along their terraced ranks with my fist clenched in celebration. That was the end of any claps I would ever receive from Celtic people except, perhaps, when I was playing for Scotland.

Matters were now coming into our own hands that April evening as we counted the games left to play – St Mirren at Pittodrie, Dundee United at Tannadice, Hibs at Easter Road and Partick Thistle at Firhill. It wasn't an easy programme but we were scenting victory and were now geared to go all out and achieve it. The Press were carrying stories that I was ill around that time and was rising from my sick bed to play. I was ill, right enough, but it was really just nerves – football players are human after all. Though I went to bed on the Friday, the boss felt it would be a psychological advantage to have me on the park against St Mirren on the Saturday. With nerves in the stomach, my ailment was diarrhoea which not only made me weak but gave rise to the crack that I was doing more running off the park than on it! We beat St Mirren with goals from Ian Scanlon and Doug Rougvie and drew with Dundee United at Tannadice on the Tuesday. That was the night, incidentally, when John McMaster and I accidentally bumped into each other at a free kick – and decided to make an act of it thereafter. I scored the equalizer.

The crucial day would now be the following Saturday, 3 May 1980, when we were due to play Hibs at Easter Road and Celtic had to go to Love Street. If we both won, it would go to the last game in midweek. If we won and Celtic only drew, Partick Thistle would have to beat us by a lot of goals to give Celtic the title.

We were apprehensive because we had not been getting results at Easter Road and this was one we simply had to win. Ian Scanlon scored twice and Steve Archibald, Andy Watson and Mark McGhee brought

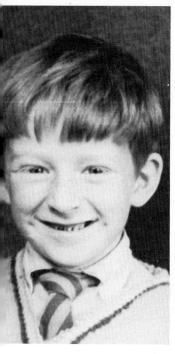

Above left: Schoolboy Strachan

Above right: A historic picture from a boys' magazine — a thirteen-year-old in the crowd at Easter Road admires his hero, Pat Stanton. The face (bottom left)? It's me!

Below: In long-haired style, with parents and sister, Laura, at Butlin's holiday camp, Ayr

Aberdeen team after winning the 1983 Scottish Cup

I've just scored the third goal in the 1982 Scottish Cup Final against Rangers

the final score to 5–0. But the match at Love Street was still in progress and we didn't know if our win would be enough to clinch the championship or not. The latest reports had been that there was no scoring. If that remained the position, Aberdeen would virtually have won the Premier League Championship for the first time since it was introduced in 1975. All round the ground people were tuned in to transistors, listening to the St Mirren–Celtic commentary. That was running more than a minute behind our match and by all accounts the score was still 0–0. Could St Mirren last out and give us our greatest dream? The crowd at Easter Road would no doubt give us our answer. Meanwhile Fergie told us to stay on the park and wave to the crowd. Next thing I knew he was flashing past me on to the park, dancing jigs of joy. A signal from Alastair Guthrie of the *Evening Express*, up in the press-box, had told him what he wanted to know – that Celtic had only drawn and that, barring an unbelievable disaster at Firhill the following week, Aberdeen had won the league title. We danced around the field receiving the acclaim of our vast army of supporters who had come to Edinburgh in anticipation of their greatest moment.

Aberdeen had won the Scottish championship only once before, in the 1954–5 season, but that happened at Shawfield Stadium, Glasgow, on a day when not many people had bothered to travel. But they were here in their thousands and on a bright, sunny day there was celebration all round. I was due to be out through suspension for the Partick Thistle game so Lesley, Gavin and I stayed on in Edinburgh for the weekend. That night we went along to the bingo at Edinburgh City Football Club and, would you believe it, I was the evening's jackpot winner. There were lots of Hibs fans there and people came crowding round to congratulate me and to say how glad they were that a club like Aberdeen had at long last cut in on the Rangers–Celtic monopoly. They were all sick of it. My dear old dad, who remains my greatest fan and allows his life to go up and down according to what I'm doing, looked at me that night and said quite dramatically, 'Son, you winning the league has been the highlight of my career!' My mother just shook her head.

We went through to Glasgow for the Partick Thistle game which ended in a 1–1 draw, a poor game and a bit of an anticlimax but it was the first time we could say officially that we were the champions of Scotland. There was more celebration going back on the bus to Aberdeen that night. I had scored fifteen goals in that memorable season. Something which needs to be said about that championship year is the part which Andy Watson played in our ultimate victory. The people who gave him a ridiculous amount of stick from the terracing soon forgot that it was the appearance of Andy in that last run-in of vital games which turned the whole league in our favour. I have never seen a footballer who worked like that boy and he kept scoring vitally important goals. He may not have been the classiest player on view but you need people like Andy in any team which has ambitions for success.

Gradually it dawned on us that that league championship would take us into the European Cup in 1980–81. Aberdeen should have been there exactly twenty-five years earlier, having won the league the very first time a Scottish club appeared in the competition. But Hibs' chairman, Harry Swan, had pioneered Scotland's entry and his club was invited as a courtesy to be Scotland's first representatives, much to the disgust of Aberdonians. Well, on Hibs' ground they had now won their ticket to Europe even if it did turn out to be so much later than it should have been.

As we left Easter Road that day, Dons fans were still celebrating out in the street. When they spotted Steve Archibald they broke into a chant of 'Don't go, Stevie!' They had been reading that his contract at Pittodrie was at an end and that Spurs were keen to buy him. It was not long before Stevie did go, but he was not alone in coming to the end of his agreement with Aberdeen. Alec

McLeish and myself were in the same position, except that there were no concrete offers for us. We were going through the business of talking about new terms and wondering whether we should sign or not. I didn't want to sign and then find that someone like Alec was leaving so he and I discussed the position and agreed that if one of us accepted a new contract the other would do so too. And that is how it happened that we committed ourselves to Aberdeen until the spring of 1984.

I was gaining my first full cap for Scotland against Northern Ireland in the home internationals, the first time the Scots had been in Belfast for many years, because of the troubles. We lost 1–0 but made good against Wales at Hampden when Willie Miller scored the only goal of the game.

After a 2–0 defeat from England we set off for Poland and Hungary, all in the build-up for the start of the qualifying stages of the World Cup in 1982. That first match was in Sweden – strange how that country kept creeping into my career – and Mr Stein was anxious to get us off to a good start. Realistically, I suppose, we were expecting no better than a draw but we came away with a famous victory which put my name on the international map. Before the match nobody seemed particularly anxious to know me but afterwards I became more popular with players, Press and everyone else as they crowded round to talk about the only goal of the game, which I had managed to score. It was the night when Archie Gemmell and I worked a double act through the Swedish defence and I found myself coming into the penalty area, on the left side, wondering if I had left myself enough of an angle from which to send the ball past the advancing keeper, Ronnie Helstroem. Luckily I got it right, the ball evading him just enough to get in at his left-hand post. It was an important game and one which I should treasure in my memory but, in fact, it was not enjoyable from a player's point of view. There was too much tension and I can remember wishing it would hurry up and finish. As consolation, the headlines next morning gave me credit for firing a 'glory goal' and setting Scotland on the road to Spain, which is how it turned out.

Back home at Pittodrie there was equally important business on hand as we embarked on our first-ever experience of the European Cup, meeting the Austrian team Memphis. In the first leg at Pittodrie we managed only a narrow lead, with a goal from Mark McGhee, and Frank Gilfeather of Grampian Television was among those who all but wrote us off for the return leg.

But we played splendidly in Austria, holding Memphis to a goal-less draw and giving poor old Frank some ribbing on the homeward journey. The only black spot on that occasion was a nasty incident in which a bus carrying Dons fans away from the game was attacked and stoned. Among those who cowered through the terrifying ordeal was Drew Jarvie's wife Janette.

Having reached the second round we couldn't have drawn a more difficult one than the reigning champions of England, Liverpool. To most people it seemed too much to expect that we would go beyond that round but there was a surprising amount of confidence in the Dons' dressing room. I would even say we were super-confident and thought we were going to beat them. The first leg at Pittodrie turned out to be a big disappointment, however. Within a few minutes Terry McDermott had scored one of the best executed goals I have seen and we began to wonder what we were playing against here. Liverpool played the ball across the field and back again in that casual way which may not be very entertaining to the spectators but which seems to be effective for clubs like that. What dampened our challenge most of all, however, was the shocking injury to John McMaster. John was starting out on one of his beautifully smooth runs, beating one man then another as he cut diagonally across the field. It looked like the start of something promising. Then in came Ray Kennedy and felled him with a knee-high tackle which not only put him out of the game for a year but raised some doubts that he would ever walk properly again, let alone play football. I am not saying Kennedy went out to crock him but if you use that kind of tackle, there is a fair chance that you will do your opponent some nasty harm.

Personally I would discourage such tackles in the strongest possible way. Justice would be best done by banning the tackler for the same length of time as the injured man is out of the game, although that would no doubt be regarded as impracticable. The incredible point about that particular tackle was that Kennedy didn't even get a booking. It was the last we saw of John McMaster for a long time and if you had seen the injury you could have understood why. With ligaments severed, his leg from the knee down was hanging away in the wrong direction. You wouldn't have believed it. I'll tell you, it made us all stop and think about how easily your career could be ended in just one tackle. Needless to say, we were all sick for John, who must surely rate as one of the finest footballers ever seen at Pittodrie.

When we went to Anfield Park, Liverpool, for the return leg on Guy Fawkes night 1980, we were still confident we could retrieve the situation of a 1–0 defeat. We started knocking the ball about quite effectively and Mark McGhee and Ian Scanlon had good chances. The Liverpool players were beginning to get ratty with each other and Graeme Souness was giving out some stick to his side. We thought we had them in our sights when big Doug Rougvie played the ball out for a corner kick. Over came the ball and Willie Miller scored an own-goal. Willie was having such a spate of own-goals around that time that he seemed in danger of becoming our top scorer! Phil Neale scored a second and we were on our way to a 4–0 defeat and an exit from our first venture into the European Cup. But even at half-time there was still a glimmer of confidence in the Dons' dressing room. The boss had come in screaming at us, especially the international players, and as we prepared to go out for the second half that great old battler, Drew Jarvie, pulled himself up in all seriousness and said, 'Right lads, three early goals and we're right back in it.'

It was the overstatement of the year and a long time afterwards Fergie confessed that, despite his explosion at half-time, he had nearly burst out laughing at Drew's optimism. The happiest memory of that evening in Liverpool was the sound made by three thousand Aberdeen fans who had made the journey south and gained a bit of fame for themselves by out-shouting the famous Kop with all its thousands. Little things stick in your memory and, with that match being sponsored by KP, I remember coming out with bags of their potato crisps and thinking they were poor consolation for being knocked out of the European Cup.

Looking back, the main consolation was the lesson we had learned – that however good we may have thought we were, there was still a long way to go before we could say we belonged up there with the best in Europe. But we were certainly on our way.

11

A Thug Attacks Me

In the preparation for the two games between Aberdeen and Liverpool, manager Bob Paisley gained a lot of newspaper space by coming to watch us in advance and saying he believed I would be the first two-million-pound player to be transferred in Britain. Some people thought it was a propaganda stunt to upset Aberdeen, blowing up my head and sending me rushing for the calculator to see what my percentage of that lot would be. But nothing like that happened.

Having only recently signed my new contract with the Dons, I just accepted his compliment and put the whole matter behind me. As things turned out, there were not going to be any two-million-pound transfers in the foreseeable future with the recession biting into most clubs' finances and taking some of them to the point of bankruptcy. The two million pounds which Bob Paisley was speaking about could be translated into something like the £750,000 which Arsenal were later to pay Celtic for Charlie Nicholas. In normal circumstances, the Nicholas figure – and maybe the one Aberdeen would have been expecting for me – would have been considerably more than the £800,000 which Spurs paid Aberdeen for Steve Archibald.

One way or another it had been quite a year, on top of which the Scottish sportswriters had voted me Scottish Player of the Year. In his encouragement of home-based players, Jock Stein said publicly:

Gordon Strachan played a major part in winning the championship for Aberdeen and when he came into the Scottish side he did all I expected of him. He settled down quickly and was not in the slightest way overawed. He is a good player in the old Scottish tradition. By that I mean he gets the ball and isn't frightened to take people on. He may be suffering a bit just now because of tighter marking but he has had a marvellous year and scored that vital goal in Sweden to give us those equally vital World Cup points.

But my dramas of 1980 were not over. Though I seemed to have had a habit of stirring up antagonism from opposition fans, especially at Ibrox and Parkhead where nobody is supposed to be as good as their players, I had not reached the stage where any of them had actually assaulted me physically. The fact that I didn't have long to wait for that moment is a sad reflection on what has happened on the terracings of football. It was in a match at Celtic Park that the campaign of hate finally spilled over to the field of play. I had gone on a run up the park, beating three or four players as I went and having a shot at goal before making my way back. I wasn't paying any particular attention to the crowd but I did happen to see a chap coming over the wall from what is known as the Jungle, where the hard core of Celtic fans stand, often chanting the most awful slogans. It seems a bit incredible now but this fellow actually passed two police officers on his way. I turned and thought I had better pay attention to Tommy Burns when I next saw this guy wandering about in the centre circle. 'Aye, aye,' I thought to myself, 'he must be looking for somebody.' He had a bottle with him but that fell out of his hand on the track. I tried to concentrate on the game but the next thing I knew he was beside me and launching his attack.

I covered my face but he got me by the neck and pulled me to the ground. A big chap he was too. Luckily Doug Rougvie and Doug Bell were smartly on hand to save me from further damage and the Celtic players came to my rescue as well. It would be nice to be able to say these incidents have no real effect on your game but things like that do achieve their purpose. I was completely shaken by the experience and might as well have come off the park after that. I was walking about in a daze. My wife, Lesley, was in the stand that day, paying her first visit to Celtic Park, so you can imagine what an impression she got of the place. Of course fans like that do their own club no good and Celtic had to pay a £1000 fine. But we are kidding ourselves if we think there is only a small minority of people who approve of that kind of action. Whereas you might have thought the fans would be ashamed of an attack like that on their home ground, I continued to get stick from the Celtic people, who gave the attacker the biggest cheer of the day as he was led away. It doesn't improve your impression of football supporters. And when it is all over, a reaction sets in and you start thinking of all the possibilities. What if he had had a knife in his hand?

Another man with a knife in his hand was not far away in my career but in totally different circumstances. By the turn of that year Aberdeen were four points clear at the top and looking set to repeat their Premier League triumph of the previous season. I was having my own minor problems with a groin strain which was not painful enough to stop me playing but was still putting me off my game.

The matter came to a head when we met Dundee United at Pittodrie and Iain Phillip and I jumped together for a ball. Suddenly I felt a tearing inside me, like the noise of cellophane ripping. I played out the game in great pain and knew right away that I was in serious trouble. With every step sheer agony, I signed to the dugout that I was incapable of doing anything. Then we were awarded a penalty and when Willie Miller asked if I could take it, I had to tell him I couldn't even walk up to the ball, let alone kick it. Ian Scanlon took the kick instead and gave us a 1–1 draw. That took place in December 1980, and I couldn't have guessed that that was to be the end of me until the following season. It began with orders to stay in bed and rest as much as I could. With no sign of improvement I started to panic and I then tried the old Chinese practice of acupuncture, with needles stuck all over my body. I had treatment from a chap who was one of the Vietnamese boat people, refugees from the war in the Far East. But nothing was working. I had the added worry that we were moving into another house in Ferryhill and I was unable to be of any help. Some days I would get out of bed like an old man and try touching my toes. It all preyed on my mind. Is this the end of my career? How are we going to live from now on? Will they give me a testimonial? Was my mother right about not depending on football as a career? While I was managing to torture myself with these thoughts, Aberdeen were slipping down the league, which people were generous enough to say had something to do with my absence.

I was also missing out on that World Cup run which had started so promisingly for me in Sweden. Actually, it was at one of those Scottish games that the first glimmer of hope appeared. Alec Ferguson had decided to go to Israel with the Scotland party and while there he was discussing me with my old buddy Steve Archibald. It was Steve who came up with the information that one of his team-mates at Tottenham, Tony Galvin, had had something similar. By March 1981, I had been out of the game for eleven weeks so Fergie came home from that trip and made arrangements for me to see the same surgeons. I was ordered to London to see a leading Harley Street man, Sir Patrick England, and returned for a second examination by one of his colleagues, Dr George Gilmour. He looked at me for only seconds before saying, 'I think we can do something for you.' I went into the London Clinic and was operated on the next morning. They had known I had a ruptured stomach but during the operation they found that that was concealing a hernia and blocked intestinal tubes. In other words, my plumbing was in a fair old mess and the only consolation as I lay there for two weeks was that the famous London

Clinic seemed a wonderful place, offering you all the prawn cocktails, smoked salmon and fillet steaks that you wouldn't normally find in a hospital. Not that I was able to enjoy those delicacies for long because something else had gone wrong with me. I had dropped from 10 stones 3 lb to 8 stones and kept falling asleep while Lesley and Steve Archibald were at my bedside. It turned out that, while waiting for the operation, I had picked up salmonella poisoning in an Aberdeen restaurant. By bad luck, the television news was full of another outbreak of salmonella in an old folks' home where five elderly people had died of it. I wouldn't have needed much convincing that I was dying too.

Gradually I got better and, even though it took three months after that marvellous operation before the pain began to go away, I finally knew that I was on the mend.

12

We Rattle Robson

The season had come and gone, with Celtic winning the championship, but now it was summer and my aim was to be playing early in the new season of 1981–2. In July I started training on my own or along with assistant manager Archie Knox, who had taken over when my old hero, Pat Stanton, went off to be a manager in his own right, finally landing up with his beloved Hibs.

I had known Archie as a player and as an opponent in his days with Dundee United. Since then he had done a good job as manager of Forfar and was now settling in as No. 2 to Fergie at Pittodrie. Whereas Pat Stanton had had a totally different style from the boss, Archie was much on the same lines, only occasionally more so. If the boss happened to miss a scream, Archie was ready to supply it. They worked well in training together, not exactly the namby-pamby types and not always agreeing, by any means. In fact they would argue and disagree quite loudly. Archie was certainly no yes-man. After a session under his command, it was a relief to get home to the peace and quiet of my own home to give my ears a break.

The saving grace of such people is that, apart from knowing the game – and we couldn't put up with them if they didn't – they often have a keen sense of humour. Archie tells a great story. What's more, since he started to be a coach he has become a much better player than ever he was in his playing days! In training he can pass a great ball.

At the start of the 1981–2 season Aberdeen arranged a pre-season tournament at Pittodrie, a glamorous affair with Manchester United, Southampton and West Ham making up a four-team contest. The Dons beat Southampton by a splendid 5–1 in the final, when I scored from a penalty. The main thing was that I was back in business and delighted just to be kicking a ball again in a competitive match for the first time in eight months. There are not too many eight-month periods in a footballer's career so it is a serious business when you are out of the game for that length of time. Anyhow, it was a fantastic feeling just to be back and that evening we held a party where I didn't need any drink to be high.

As the season got under way the immediate excitement was going to be our double meeting with Ipswich Town, who had reached their moment of European glory at the end of the previous season by winning the UEFA Cup. They went into the hat automatically as reigning champions and some folk thought it unfortunate that we had drawn them in the first round. However, any idea that we would not stand much of a chance against them had to be set against the fact that Ipswich were a club of much the same standing as Aberdeen, not perhaps one of the glamour names of English football but drawing on the same kind of population as ourselves, with the same kind of resources and having built themselves into a position where they had gone out with some honest hard work and won a cup in Europe. It could be done – as Aberdonians were to know at a later date. So we went south to Portman Road on 16 September for the first leg of our UEFA Cup first-round tie and took everybody by surprise, holding Ipswich to a 1–1 draw.

The Aberdeen players were disappointed that they had not grabbed their chances and finished the tie there and then. As it was, we had to settle for level scoring, our goal coming from that young man of vital moments, John Hewitt. Ipswich manager Bobby Robson, showing some of that arrogance for which his nation has been known, said he did not believe Aberdeen could play better than they did at Portman Road and therefore he was confident of stepping up his team's performance and winning through to the second round at Pittodrie. We knew better.

Pittodrie was buzzing with anticipation that night of the return match, 30 September, the crowd wondering if we could pull off the shock of the tournament by knocking out the Cup holders on our home ground. The atmosphere was tremendous. In the first half I robbed John Wark of the ball in his own penalty area and he turned and pulled me down. I scored from the spot. Wark himself equalized from another penalty before half-time and that was how it stood at the interval. Out we came, all square and determined that we were going to make it a memorable night for the Dons fans. Peter Weir, who was beginning to shake off a complex about having cost the club around £300,000, turned on one of those superb performances and put us in the lead. Then Fergie produced one of his master strokes. Of all the Aberdeen players that Robson had been studying, he didn't know much, if anything, about an amazing guy called Dougie Bell. The boss put him on as substitute, knowing that Dougie revels in the big occasion and can hold a ball and tease and torment an opposing defence as well as any man in the game today.

The more he ran at Ipswich, trailing the ball away to the corner flag, the more I knew we were now in command. On the away-goal principle, Ipswich needed only to equalize to go through on a score of 2–2 and Robson was reported to have said at the press conference after the match that he was still confident of that happening with just ten minutes to go. But he reckoned without Peter Weir, who performed an action replay of his first goal, ran straight at full back Mick Mills, jinking in that way of Peter's and putting Mills in two minds about where he was going. Mills back-pedalled as Peter cut towards his inside, always afraid that he would suddenly sprint down his outside flank. Peter kept his cool, gave himself a clearance with Mills off balance and rammed home a third goal which was going to write the next morning's headlines. The holders of the UEFA Cup had been sensationally knocked out in the first round by Aberdeen. By who? If they were asking that question on the Continent next morning they were at least beginning to know that such a team existed, a piece of knowledge that was going to come in handy in years to come. Beating Ipswich, with their big names like Paul Mariner, Mick Mills, Alan Brazil, John Wark and Eric Gates, was all the more a psychological boost to us because there was little doubt that Ipswich and Liverpool were the two best teams in England at that time. We may not have mastered Liverpool but a year later we had grown sufficiently in stature to show that we were at last beginning to bat in that class. We couldn't wait for the draw. Out of the hat came Arges Pitesti of Romania who appeared at Pittodrie for the first-leg match on 21 October 1981.

I scored the opening goal from a John McMaster cross in eleven minutes and Peter Weir and John Hewitt made it 3–0, which should have seen us comfortably through the tie. In the return match, however, Arges had snatched a 2–0 lead by half-time and were now breathing down our necks. That was the occasion I mentioned earlier, when the tea-urn went flying in the dressing room! Fergie was having one of his more dramatic moments. Just after the re-start I scored from a penalty to ease the pressure and that man Hewitt headed an equalizer five minutes from time to give us a draw over there and a comfortable 5–2 win over all.

That brought us to the third round and if Ipswich were now out of the way the favourites to win the trophy would surely be our next opponents, the famous Hamburg team, with names like the immortal millionaire, Franz Beckenbauer, a survivor of the World Cup final of 1966 but still the most cool and controlled footballer in the world in his mid-thirties. Big nights were now becoming a habit at Pittodrie. First there had been Liverpool, then Ipswich, now the great Hamburg and the crowds rolled in with hopes of seeing a memorable game. Making his debut in Europe, Eric Black opened the scoring in twenty-three minutes before an appalling mix-up between Jim Leighton and Stuart Kennedy let the Germans equalize. However Andy Watson put us back in the lead and Aberdeen began to produce what I still believe to be the finest performance of any team I have ever played in. The only performance to rival it came later, in the Olympic Stadium in Munich, but I have never known as good a show of attacking football as Aberdeen produced at Pittodrie that night. The fact that the result ended up as a shambles at 3–2 for us only made it all the more tragic that we lost goals as we did.

First of all I missed a penalty before John Hewitt made good my lapse by making it 3–1. We were just thinking it should have been about 5–1 or 6–1 when big Doug Rougvie was injured and we stupidly played on as he lay there instead of putting the ball out of the park to let the big man have attention. The Germans took advantage of the situation and punished us with a second goal which put us in a precarious position for the return game in Hamburg. That was how it turned out, Hamburg winning the second leg and putting us out by the odd goal in nine. We had been so near to a famous victory.

By my own standards I had a poor game that night. I knew it myself but even if I hadn't I would certainly have heard about it in the lashing which Fergie gave me at the Press conference afterwards. I had a few beers and some sleeping tablets to try and forget about it but I was walking through the airport like a zombie next morning. I didn't think I deserved the slanging which the boss had given me and the matter troubled me so much that I decided it was maybe time to move on. I would ask for a transfer. So I went to his office to put my case for a move. His dismissal must qualify for the shortest one on record. He just said, 'No chance. Cheerio!' And slammed the door.

I turned to face a closed door and said, 'That's very nice of you, boss.' But he wasn't there.

Then the big freeze-up came and football was out of business for weeks on end. That gave me a welcome break and sparked off what I believe to have been the best spell in my playing career.

From the early spring of 1982 through the World Cup and into the 1982–3 season seemed to me the best football I have ever played. During that weather break I trained hard and came back to football with a new appetite.

13

The Rout of Rangers

When I look back from our greatest triumph of Gothenburg 1983 and wonder where it all started, I arrive at Fir Park, Motherwell, on a winter's day of 1982 when we played the first round of the Scottish Cup which eventually took us into Europe. That was the day when Aberdeen created something of a record by scoring in nine seconds. How appropriate that the man who set us on our way with that goal at Motherwell was the same John Hewitt who finished it off at Gothenburg. You can't keep him out of it, can you? While that goal took us through, I have cause to remember the Motherwell game for the fact that I was crocked early on by a big raw lad called Forbes. A little later, another Motherwell player 'kneed' me in the back. The crowd were howling that I was faking it but I was injured all right, so much so that I didn't appear after the interval. I'm told that there were a few die-hards on the terracing still shouting abuse at me in the second half, apparently unaware that I wasn't even on the park!

Well you can perhaps excuse some mindless morons who have sawdust where their brains should be but I was appalled to find that at least one well-known journalist had the gall on the Monday morning to join in the suggestion that I was feigning injury. I couldn't believe what was being written. I wonder how a scribe, safely tucked up in his press-box, would have coped with the kind of brutality which came my way that afternoon. Anyway, I took to bathing my leg in the North Sea late at night so that nobody would see me. We were trying to keep quiet about the extent of the injury.

Lesley used to drive me down to the promenade at Aberdeen beach and I can tell you that wading into the noisy sea in darkness is a petrifying experience.

Much too early in that cup run we were drawn against Celtic but, on the basis that you have to meet the big ones sometime, we were at least lucky that the tie was at Pittodrie. I have never been so nervous in the build-up to any game. Celtic had beaten us the week before in the league, in which we didn't seem to be going anywhere that season, so we knew that this was the crunch. If we didn't win our season was finished. I couldn't drive along the street without having that game uppermost in my mind. At night I was tossing and turning, just thinking about it. That was the longest week of my life. Alec McLeish took a midfield role that day and the match itself will be remembered as the one in which John Hewitt scored with his famous overhead kick to give us victory with the only goal of the game. The way John was scoring those goals didn't really surprise me after what I had seen of the lad from the first day I came to Aberdeen. I reckoned he would be the first million-pound player to leave Scotland, such was his tremendous skill. With that talent, he should have been commanding games. Instead, he was sometimes a bit dozy, which was his only fault. But he could score goals in the highest company and his number of vital ones, as I have mentioned already, was becoming incredible. As we all know, he wasn't finished then.

That Celtic game had been a pretty hard and gruelling business and afterwards there was a story circulating to the effect that Danny McGrain burst into our dressing room and went for me. It was nonsense, of course, and I shared a joke about it with Danny later.

That is not to say there was no bad blood running between the Aberdeen and Celtic players after the match. I missed the details but as we came down the tunnel there was a commotion and I could hear shouts of

'Away you —— bastards!' The pressure of important matches like that certainly causes friction and the fact that we all meet each other so often in the Premier League and in cup games means you are liable to get feuds which are carried on from match to match. Personally I get on very well with most of our opponents. Of course there are exceptions. In the quarterfinals of the Scottish Cup that year we were drawn against Kilmarnock, again at Pittodrie. Frankly, I thought Killie had a bit of rough justice that day when we were awarded two penalties and I scored them both. On the first occasion I thought I was pulled down outside the box but the referee thought otherwise and awarded a penalty.

Well, this particular player seemed to hold me responsible for the decision, coming up to me and shouting that the foul had been outside the box. I asked him what I could do about it. Down Kilmarnock way they produce giants and call them footballers. I think they stick them in manure and grow them in greenhouses. This player was taking things in hand out there and he was going to 'do' me after the match and he was going to 'do' the boss as well. When I reached the club tearoom, where families and guests congregate after the match, I found Lesley near to tears. The Kilmarnock players had been sitting near her and this one had been vowing that he was going to break my —— leg.

A woman accompanying the Kilmarnock party apparently joined in with abuse and my wife was in quite a state. The player had no right to be behaving like that in the tearoom and when I arrived I picked up the gist of his threat. Apparently if nobody else broke my leg before next season, he would do it. I chipped in with the remark that he would be too slow to catch me and finally big Doug Rougvie had to step in and tell him to shut his face. The big fellow is handy in situations like that.

If we got a break with that penalty goal against Kilmarnock I thought we got another with our equalizing penalty goal against St Mirren in the semifinal at

Celtic Park. The saving grace of that one was that we certainly didn't deserve to lose the match. It went to a replay at Dens Park, Dundee, where we won 3–2, with goals by Mark McGhee, Neil Simpson and Peter Weir.

So to the Scottish Cup Final which would decide whether or not we played in the European Cup Winners' Cup in 1982–3. It was quite a week altogether. On the Wednesday before the match I had to rush Lesley to Fonthill Hospital where Craig was born within minutes of her arrival. On the Thursday we were putting in a spot of training at Cruden Bay when Alec McLeish got possession on the edge of the penalty-box and scooped a neat, curving shot into the far corner of the net. It looked good at the time but we soon forgot about it as we headed for Glasgow and the Cup Final against Rangers.

With their large following cheering them on, the Ibrox side were looking dangerous, Davie Cooper causing us problems as he roamed about the field. They may have thought they were on their way to yet another cup triumph when John McDonald put them into the lead. But it was short-lived. Suddenly, who popped up to gain possession on the edge of the penalty area but Alec McLeish. I was shouting for the ball. But no – big Alec was remembering Cruden Bay. With an action replay of his goal on the Aberdeenshire coast, he sent the ball into the far corner of the net and we were back on level terms. Although normal time ended at 1–1, there was no doubt in my mind that we were going to win. I put a through ball to Mark McGhee who headed us into the lead and from then on it was going to be Aberdeen's day. I had bloodied my nose but nothing seemed to matter when Mark McGhee jinked along the by-line in that special fashion of his, caused Alec Miller to seize up before nutmegging John McClelland and slipping the ball through to me. There I was with a clear view to tap the ball in; but goalmouths do funny things when you are in that position. Because you know it would be unthinkable for you to miss, the area of goalposts seems to close right

81

in on you. However I managed to squeeze it in and to do a somersault, bloodied nose and all. We were on the rampage now and the fourth and final goal had a touch of comedy about it, at least from our point of view. That exiled Aberdonian, Colin Jackson, was trying to pass back to the Rangers keeper, Jim Stewart, but the ball was never going to reach him. Stewart ran out in an attempt to clear but belted it against Neale Cooper's stomach. As Stewart was running one way, the ball was rebounding back towards his own goal and there was young Neale, a bit bewildered by the speed of events and wondering where the ball was really going.

He charged on, however, to take advantage of his good luck and to thrash the ball into the net for our fourth. By then the Rangers fans were streaming home and the glory of Hampden belonged to the red and white scarves of Aberdeen, who were due a Scottish Cup win. After their first win in 1947 they had to wait another twenty-three years for it to happen again. That was when Martin Buchan captained the Dons to victory against Celtic in 1970. Now another twelve years had passed but we had done it in style. In 1947 the score had been 2–1, in 1970 it was 3–1, but we had topped them both in 1982 by making it 4–1, even if we were the only ones to need extra time.

Two events arising from that match stand out in my mind. When I scored that third goal and did my somersault of joy, an Aberdeen supporter in Balmedie, who hadn't managed to go to Hampden, followed my example and somersaulted across his living-room. Unfortunately he banged against his stone fireplace – and broke his leg! I heard about it and visited him the following Tuesday.

The other memory belongs to Gleneagles Hotel where we went for our celebration afterwards. While people were asking for our autographs, my room-mate, Stuart Kennedy, was camping outside the hotel restaurant waiting for someone else's autograph. Stuart is a keen film buff and his all-time hero is Burt Lancaster. Imagine his excitement when he discovered that Lancaster was a fellow guest, having gone to Gleneagles for a holiday after finishing his part in *Local Hero*, which had been filmed on the West Coast and across at the village of Pennan in Aberdeenshire.

So there was Stuart in his element, finally catching up with his hero, having his picture taken with him and astonishing him with lines from his films which showed that our boy really knew his stuff. The boss allowed a few of us to go down to Auchterarder for a couple of beers and we ended up playing snooker.

That season just gone had not been without further incident on the field. If some football supporters had learned to dislike me it bubbled over again when we met Celtic at Pittodrie in a league match. We were awarded a penalty at the Paddock end, which housed the visiting fans at that time. It is amazing how you can see the hate on the faces of people behind a goal who are willing you to miss the penalty chance. After all the obscenities, however, it is a great feeling to score and once again I celebrated with a somersault. The boys gathered round to congratulate me when I saw another of those idiots coming on to the park to get me. He barged into the group but I was saved by the lads.

During that season, too, I had nominated Tom Aitken, the Edinburgh janitor who first spotted me, to present me with the Mackinlay's Personality of the Month award. It was fitting to have Tom there. In his little speech he said, 'Gordon was a born player. It was obvious, even at the age of nine, that he had the talent to make a big name for himself and I'm delighted he has done so.' I was just as delighted Tom was there to receive some credit for whatever I had achieved. During that past season too, Sunderland manager Alan Durban said he had made an approach for me but had been met by a 'brick wall' at the club.

Oddly enough Durban had offered, as part exchange,

two players our boss had previously been keen to sign, Iain Munro, formerly of St Mirren, and Ally McCoist, who went from St Johnstone and was later to return to join Rangers.

14

Enter James Bond

Having just won the Scottish Cup and qualified for
Europe, the Aberdeen contingent joined up the following
week for the Wales and England matches. When we
played England at Hampden, I was on the bench and
those same Rangers fans who could have strung me up
the previous week were chanting my name like some kind
of hero. It's a funny business football! Anyway, chants or
no chants Jock Stein did not give in to their demands and
said he was keeping me for the opening World Cup
match against New Zealand. Having missed out on some
of the qualifying matches because of that long injury, I
had finally made it back into the international squad in
time to play in the last stages before going to Spain for
the World Cup proper. I would dearly have loved to be
on the field against England that day at Hampden
because I knew I was playing my best-ever football but I
bowed to Mr Stein's judgement and was all excited as we
set out for Portugal, in preparation for Spain. We flew to
the Algarve and settled into the luxury of the Penina Golf
Hotel, home of Henry Cotton's golf school, where I
managed a few rounds with Paul Sturrock and George
Burley.

I was also getting to know Jock Stein a lot better and
to realize that he treated us like men more than we were
accustomed to at club level.

He had not always been able to trust his international
squads to behave themselves but he seemed to have
every faith in us and didn't mind if we had a pint or two

as long as we kept our heads and didn't start doing stupid things. He can be quite a funny man and enjoys a great rapport with Jimmy Steel, the physiotherapist who comes along with the Scottish party and is worth his weight in gold. Jimmy is a real comedian whose patter keeps the boys going. Now in his late sixties, he still bursts into hilarious impersonations of Hitler and can have a whole party in stitches. A great bloke. With him and Jock getting on so well together, you have no idea how much an atmosphere like that can improve morale. At Penina, Stein didn't talk much about tactics. While we were getting into the right frame of mind he allowed the Press reasonable scope to come and talk to us. But there came a time when he knew that enough was enough and his authority was complete. The Press just quietly disappeared.

Our excitement began to mount as we moved across the border from Portugal into Spain, scene of the 1982 World Cup Finals, and took up residence at the Tennis Hotel in Sotogrande, just round the corner from Gibraltar. From then on it was a steady build-up to our first World Cup game against New Zealand at La Rosaleda Stadium in Malaga on 15 June. When that night arrived it was so humid I felt we could have done with a blast of Aberdeen air but at least the pitch was in such perfect condition you could have played bowls on it.

I had now played twelve times for Scotland and I felt myself getting right into this game. With just over a quarter of an hour gone I gained possession and started on a long run, warding off challenges until I reached the penalty area. Then I pushed the ball through to Kenny Dalglish – and we were one up. I knew I was on song that night. Next I picked up a ball from Danny McGrain and pushed a short pass to Alan Brazil whose shot rebounded off the New Zealand keeper – and there was John Wark lying handy to send the ball back into the net. We looked unstoppable. Again I gained possession away out on the right, spotted John Wark making a run down the left and swung over a long ball which he met with his head for our third goal.

With that comfortable half-time lead we should have been set for a high score but it is in that kind of situation that we Scots have a habit of letting ourselves down. Nine minutes after the interval Danny McGrain and Alan Rough both hesitated and in stepped Sumner to pull one back for New Zealand. Inspired by their goal, they became more adventurous and, lo and behold, they scored a second. You would think at times that Scotland like to see how many silly goals they can give away while still winning the game. It didn't look too clever now that we were leading just 3–2 in a match where there could have been a runaway score. During training we were working out some set pieces when Jim McLean, the Dundee United manager who was Jock Stein's assistant, said, 'You boys at Aberdeen have some good ideas for free kicks. What about trying them out for Scotland?' So we told him the one where two players seem to argue in front of the ball then suddenly they separate and a third player chips it over the defensive wall towards the corner of the net.

We practised that one and were delighted that the opportunity arose when we were struggling to regain command of a game which had slipped away from us. That was when John Robertson chipped a perfect ball into the left-hand corner of the goal to put us 4–2 up. Finally I took a corner on the right and Steve Archibald, who had come on for Brazil, headed us to a full-time score of 5–2. When I was taken off before the end I had run myself into the ground and felt so shattered I could hardly draw breath. Dave Narey went on in my place, delighted to be chalking up another cap. I knew the Spanish crowd had taken to me that night and I came off to loud applause and was later voted Man of the Match.

When we got back to the hotel we were in the sitting room watching another World Cup match on television when I was conscious of this man beside me, with smoke belching from his cigarette. It was annoying me and I was on the point of asking him to put out the cigarette when I suddenly realized the smoker was none other than James Bond. Yes, Sean Connery lives down that coast, near Marbella, and being the enthusiastic Scot that he is, he was there to meet and encourage us all he could. He and I got talking, two Edinburgh men together, and I soon forgot all about his smoke. If we had gone beyond the initial stages of the World Cup he was offering us a different kind of accommodation on that coast where he is so well connected. Earlier that day, some of us had called on that fervent supporter of Scottish football, Rod Stewart, who also had a villa outside Marbella.

The second of the three games in our group was due three days later, on Friday 18 June, at the Benito Villamarin Stadium in Seville, which is well away from the coast. As we stepped off the bus it was like the heat of an oven hitting us in the face. If we had started well against the Kiwis, we seemed set to carry on the habit against Brazil when big Dave Narey shot us into the lead. I think we were all a bit stunned and trying to convince ourselves that we were actually a goal ahead against the great Brazilians. We were then playing it tight, I suppose trying to hold on to what we had in the belief that we might never be in front of them again. Personally I believe we should have been driving forward in search of a second goal. You never know, we might have got it. On the other hand, that might have given them the kind of opening they can snap up before you know what has happened. Before half-time Zico equalized with one of those bending, dipping shots that only men of that calibre can dispatch. Alan Rough was criticized for not reaching it but criticism was totally out of order. The ball went over my head by four or five feet and I would have sworn it was going high over the bar. But these chaps seem to have a remote control over their shots and suddenly it dipped down and into the far corner of the net. I defy any goalkeeper to anticipate a shot like that. I thought I spotted a weakness at left back and I was telling John Robertson to try long balls to John

Wark's head at that left-back spot. In just three minutes after the interval, however, full-back Oscar had put the Brazilians ahead and Eder and Falcao made the final score 4−1. Alan Rough came in for criticism when Eder chipped a ball neatly passed him but again that was quite unfair. If a Scot had scored that one we would have been claiming it as the goal of the century.

Eder had been blasting hard shots throughout the game then all of a sudden he came up with this beautifully delicate chip. I knew long before the end that we were playing against the best footballing side in the world and I wouldn't have missed the experience for anything. When you compare that to a normal club game you realize that the different levels of football are poles apart. I was left with one outstanding impression of that match with Brazil. It was the fact that, while we in this country play from fear, always looking at the dugout and wondering what criticism is coming next, those South Americans get on with their game and play from joy. In fact they spread such a feeling of happiness in their play that we were almost inclined to join in their celebrations!

So we came to the third and final game in our section, against the Russians, a game we had to win if we were to qualify for the last stages. The Russian goalkeeper had a fantastic game that night as we battled to score the winning goal. With just six minutes to go the score stood at 1−1 and there was always the chance that we could snatch the winner and go through to the last sixteen for the first time ever. That chance seemed to have gone completely when Alan Hansen and our own Willie Miller got in each other's way and left the ball breaking kindly to a Russian who had only to run on and beat Alan Rough. The Hansen−Miller incident happened away out on the touchline and should not have caused any problems at all, but it sparked off a great argument as to who was at fault. With Hansen facing his own goal and Miller heading away from it, the majority verdict was that Willie was at least going in the right direction.

Putting my Aberdeen bias aside, however, I must admit I thought they were both at fault because nobody took command of the situation and shouted 'It's mine!'

In the end, I suppose, Willie Miller can point to the fact that Hansen was later dropped from the Scottish team while he marched on to become established at the centre of the defence and to take over as captain when necessary. Once Alan Rough was faced with that advancing Russian the only way he could possibly have stopped him was to commit the so-called professional foul, grabbing him by the legs. It would not have been ethical though I can think of some goalkeepers who would have grabbed wherever they could. If Alan had pulled him down and prevented that goal he would no doubt have been hailed a national hero. If he had been a Spanish keeper doing that to a Scot, he would have been branded a thug. So often in football it depends what side you are on. Of course that wasn't the end of the Russian game. Graeme Souness came storming back to shoot a splendid equalizer. But there was no time left to try for that winning goal and it was a galling thought that we had failed to reach that very last stage by a difference of one.

It was another opportunity to blame Scotland for once again failing at the last hurdle. Realistically we should maybe consider that, for a nation of just five million people, it is a bit of an impertinence expecting to be there at all. We do remarkably well in world-class football, especially when you remember that, while we have qualified for the last three World Cups, our neighbours in England, with ten times our population, managed to get through in 1982 for the first time in their own right since they qualified twenty years earlier. I suffered disappointment for only an hour after that Russian game. I had a meal with my parents, interrupted by journalists and fans crowding round for interviews and autographs and suddenly I just wanted to get back to Aberdeen.

A month was a long time and I hadn't seen little Craig

since he was a week old. So I headed home with treasured memories of my first World Cup. The Spanish Press voted me the best player in our section, which was quite an honour when you thought of other players like Brazil's Zico in the same group. I was also voted into the World XI. It had always been my ambition to play in the World Cup and now my thoughts were cast ahead to the next one in 1986, when I would still be in my twenties and hopefully capable of holding my place in the Scottish team. The Spanish evidently likened me to Neranjito, their World Cup mascot. Maybe it was the red hair that did it but they christened me 'Little Orange.'

15

A 'Coo' in Albania

I arrived home from the World Cup after a year of almost continuous football feeling tired and suffering a bit from the anticlimax. The experience of Spain had opened my eyes to a football world beyond our own domestic league and it had the effect of unsettling me. Just as I had set my sights at first on playing for a top Scottish club and then on playing for Scotland, I was beginning to stretch my horizons again, encouraged by the fact that, without seeming bigheaded I hope, I did not seem out of place among some of the best players in the world.

I was in that kind of mood when an *Evening Express* reporter, Ian Campbell, came to interview me and I told him I was intending to ask for a transfer. I thought I couldn't face another season of playing those same teams I had been seeing for nearly ten years, meeting the same tea ladies, eating the same pies and listening to the same obscenities and threats. The *Evening Express* article was due in the paper on the Monday but when I mentioned my feelings to the boss he said to come up to his house on the Sunday and we would discuss it over a couple of beers. I began to think it was maybe unwise to be asking for a transfer and that the boss would probably talk me out of it anyway. Aberdeen had been good to me and I should just play out my contract as intended. Then I had a call from the *Evening Express* on the Saturday to say the article was on its way into the paper that day. It was too late to stop it. The boss read it and didn't waste any time

More action from the 1982 Scottish Cup Final

Above: Putting a punch into my work at the Rosslyn sports shop

Below left: I come off second-best in a tussle with Ray Kennedy in Aberdeen's European Cup tie with Liverpool at Pittodrie

Below right: With my fellow conspirator in dead-ball situations, John McMaster

A familiar scene — I've been chopped again!

Doug Bell pulls off a Celtic fan who has come to attack me on the pitch at Pittodrie

I score the only goal in the World Cup match in Sweden in 1980 — the one which set Scotland on the way to Spain

Below left: A bunch of sharp-shooters dress up on their way home from Scotland's tour of Canada in 1983: Roy Aitken, myself, Tommy Burns and Mark McGhee

Below right: Discussion with that great man of Pittodrie, Teddy Scott

in reaching me.

I was actually in a shop in Aberdeen buying a pair of shoes when he tracked me down and phoned the shop! Let's say he wasn't exactly in a mood for congratulations and I think he was quite right to take the attitude he did. I had acted hastily and regretted it soon afterwards. The whole thing fizzled out and the boss and I are still the best of mates.

People say home-based Scots become unsettled when they mix with their international team-mates from England and hear all the talk of big money. I can honestly say that has never been the case with me. You don't need to mix with them to know what they earn. You can read it in the papers any day. It is common knowledge that a Bryan Robson or a Charlie Nicholas earns about £2000 a week. I don't deny that it can sometimes be annoying to know that you earn so much less when you perhaps feel you are just as good a player. But that's life. I try to take a sensible view of it and remember that not too many of them will be able to show their grandchildren a European Cup Winners' Cup medal. After the World Cup I just knew I needed a change of scenery and, according to newspaper reports, the clubs who were after me included Valencia, Southampton, Tottenham Hotspur, Arsenal, Barcelona, Juventus and Nantes. But there were still two years of my contract to run and Laurie McMenemy of Southampton turned instead to David Armstrong of Middlesbrough and paid £750,000 for him, the kind of money Aberdeen would certainly have been accepting for me a year later. Spurs were supposed to have offered a million pounds and Fergie was said to have scared them off with talk of two million. Spurs assistant manager, Peter Shreeve, was quoted as saying that, in the current financial climate, 'there is no way we can afford that class of player.'

The great Eusebio of Portugal was not exactly running me down either. He said, 'Strachan's play in the World Cup excited me. He is one of the finest players I have seen in years. I had heard the name of Gordon Strachan before but did not know he was that good. He was better than some of the Brazilians.' Heaping more embarrassment on my head, Belgian boss Guy Thys said he fancied me more than Diego Maradona, which seemed to stretch it a bit far since he is probably the best player in the world today.

I kept my feet on the ground and got down to playing my football for Aberdeen, knowing that we were set to appear in the European Cup Winners' Cup. As one of the lesser sides in the competition we were forced to play a preliminary round against FC Sion of Switzerland at the very start of the new season, 1982–3. This 'rabbit' status which forced us to prove ourselves before we joined the first round proper was something we would have to change. We set about it in the right frame of mind, determined to show that we didn't belong in that lower bracket. The Swiss came to Pittodrie for the first leg on 13 August and we proceeded to thrash them 7–0 in a thoroughly professional performance which left the second leg as nothing but a formality. I was nevertheless quite excited about going to Switzerland, a country I had never seen, and I was not disappointed. The Tourbillon Stadium was in a beautifully picturesque setting, lying in a valley with mountains rising to snowcapped peaks and villages dotted above us like dolls' houses. The fact that some of us spent the first ten minutes admiring the magnificent view did not prevent us from adding a 4–1 score to our first one.

Now that we had arrived at the first round we found ourselves drawn against Dinamo Tirana of Albania, a country not exactly popular with visiting footballers and journalists. Their totalitarian state makes it very difficult to know anything about your opponents in advance so Fergie had to give up any idea of spying them out. For all we knew it could have been a team of seven-foot giants who were coming to Pittodrie for the first leg. They turned out to be a very fit side, with a lot of man-to-man marking but nothing more than moderate by European standards. It was a frustrating night for the 15,000 fans as the Albanian goalmouth underwent a steady bombardment and enjoyed a charmed existence. Finally the Tirana goalkeeper failed to hold a Doug Bell shot which rebounded from his chest and John Hewitt was there to score. The fact that a one-goal lead is never a satisfactory margin to carry on a foreign journey was all the more annoying when you considered that they were really not a team of any class and should have been well beaten in Aberdeen.

When we headed to the unknown territory of Albania two weeks later we could not have guessed that there would be a lot more drama outside the stadium than inside it. The folks back home were hearing more about it on radio and television then we were in Tirana. The substance of it was that, on the day of the match, there was an attempted coup, with the son of the former king trying to make a comeback with a landing on the beach. Bullets were flying about and the landing party was later reported to have been shot.

During the game we were thinking twice about putting in a real tackle in case somebody might think about getting trigger-happy with us. There was a 20,000 crowd in the Qemal Stafa Stadium and the Albanians proved to be very pleasant hosts. One of their players, Gega, kept coming up to shake my hand and wanting to pose for pictures – before kicking me halfway round the park and getting himself booked for his trouble. The hotel was clean but we took our own food just in case. They had left Communist propaganda in our rooms but, in contrast to some other Communist countries I have visited where you see big, flashy cars, most people did seem to be confined to a modest bicycle. In the streets the only thing they wanted from us was chocolate. Meanwhile the Scottish journalists were having difficulty in getting their reports transmitted back home, not an unusual happening in Albania we were told, and the lack of information was causing some concern among our families, in view of the news about the coup.

95

When somebody told Neil Simpson there was a coup, he said in his typically Northeast style, 'A coo? The only coo I can see is ower in 'at park.' As for the match itself, we held them to a no-scoring draw and were relieved to be heading back home in safety, with the prospect of another European round just ahead of us.

With so many big names of European football still in the competition, the sound of Lech Poznan of Poland didn't cause great excitement among our supporters when it came out of the hat in the draw for the next round. That was reflected in the 18,000 crowd which turned up at Pittodrie on 20 October 1982, for the first leg of our second-round tie, the furthest that Aberdeen ever seemed to go in Europe.

If people had known more about Polish football and Lech Poznan in particular they might have been ready to attach more importance to a decent result against them. Apart from the fact that Poland had reached the semifinals of the World Cup in Spain, Lech Poznan were on their way to winning the Polish league championship that season. A team below them in the league knocked Liverpool out of Europe so we should all have been more impressed with what was about to take place. They were big, strong lads, those Poles, but we set about them with determination and Mark McGhee put us ahead. Then I had a good run to the penalty area and crossed for Peter Weir to sidefoot the ball into the net.

Two weeks later we set out for the troubled land of Poland wondering if a two-goal margin would be enough to carry us through to the quarterfinals. We had all read about the Polish people's struggle and seen it on television and most of us took several pounds worth of chocolate which we gave away to the children. The youngsters' appreciation of the chocolate was matched by the adults' appreciation of the football. There were 30,000 people inside the Bulgarska Stadium. They obviously recognized the Aberdeen players they had seen in the World Cup and were prepared to give us a very fair reception. Both teams played well in the first half but

Jim Leighton was dealing very confidently with anything that came his way and we could sense that the Poles were losing heart as they struggled to break down our defence and get the goals they needed to be level. Then Doug Bell, that remarkable dynamo of a player, got into his stride and scored for the Dons. That made the Polish task impossible and reminded us again of what a tremendous player the former St Mirren man really is. He is perpetual motion once he starts and when the rest of us are panting in an exhausting game he runs on as fresh as a daisy and afraid of no one.

Great names and reputations mean nothing to him. They only inspire him to turn on his best performances and to demonstrate more of that close control which never ceases to amaze me. If only he would vary his play a little, Dougie Bell would be a Scottish internationalist tomorrow.

When we woke up that following morning, 4 November 1982, it was to realize that Aberdeen were through to the last eight of a European competition for the first time in fifteen years of trying. Yes, we were in the quarterfinals of the European Cup Winners' Cup and there was a sense of pride among the lads that we had created our own bit of history for Aberdeen Football Club by getting that far. What's more, we had done it in style, having won our away tie as well as our home one without the loss of a goal.

16

Magic of Munich

The draw for the quarterfinals of the Cup Winners' Cup was five weeks away and the ties themselves would not be played until the following March. But the buzz which keeps players on their toes was now beginning. We studied the teams still left in the tournament – Real Madrid, Barcelona, Inter Milan, Bayern Munich, four of the greatest names in world club football. The others were Paris St Germain, Austria Wien and Waterschei of Belgium, not as glamorous as the others but tough opponents just the same. Having got this far, could we possibly go any further?

Of one thing we were certain. Aberdeen tended to play better football against the better teams so we really had no worries about who would come out of the hat that December day. You had to beat them all in the end although it was sometimes tempting to think that a lesser opponent might improve your chances of reaching the semifinal.

All the guessing was over on 9 December when word came through that we had been drawn against the great Bayern Munich. What a story that name conjures up. European Cup Winners for three years running – 1974, 1975, 1976; World Club Champions in 1976; winners of the European Cup Winners' Cup in 1967; just beaten in the last European Cup Final by Aston Villa. The club which produced World Cup immortals like Franz Beckenbauer and Gerd Muller and now had great names like

Karl-Heinz Rummenigge (twice European Player of the Year), Paul Breitner, Wolfgang Dremmler, Dieter Hoeness and Jean-Marie Pfaff.

The Dons' players welcomed the draw because we knew and understood German football and knew that Bayern's amazing record of success on their home ground was achieved by skill and not by the thuggery and villainy you can encounter among the Latins. We knew the Germans would not resort to spitting and all the other dirty tricks you can come across in some of those continental teams. If we played well enough it would be possible to win in Munich, whereas victory on a Spanish or Italian ground would be near to impossible. For a start, the referees are scared of the crowds.

From the date of the draw the match was still three months away and every player at Pittodrie was gearing himself to being part of that occasion. Nobody could afford to drop their form. Everybody would pray that they would avoid injury. The league programme was just approaching the halfway stage and we were very much in contention there, along with Celtic and Dundee United. The players had to keep their minds on the home front with the European game as a carrot in the distance. Little did I know that I was soon to hit the headlines on two counts. The first was a report in the *Sunday Mail* by Allan Herron, saying that Bayern Munich were preparing a million-pound bid to take me to Germany as a replacement for Paul Breitner, who was planning to retire at the end of the season. The boss was furious and naturally so. He condemned it as pre-match gamesmanship in an attempt to unsettle Aberdeen before the two teams met a few weeks later. It appeared that someone posing as an agent had 'offered' me to Bayern and their boss, Uli Hoeness, was misled into thinking I was available. When he discovered I was still on contract for another eighteen months he conceded that I couldn't become a Bayern player. But he confirmed his genuine interest. I never discovered the identity of the mystery agent. But the incident did give rise to a lot of banter around Pittodrie where I became known as 'Hermann' or just 'Herr Strachan.'

The other matter which gained public attention was more serious. In our league match against Rangers I sustained a hamstring injury, one of the worst in football, and faced up to the fact that I would be out of the game for six weeks. That was a blow. While the rest of the lads were building themselves up for the big date in Europe, I was resigned to a strain which would take its own good time to heal. It is difficult to keep up your morale in a situation like that. Football is a game of such ups and downs that I doubt if the average supporter stops to think about how the players are affected. Just a few months earlier I had been on top of the world, hailed for my performances in the World Cup. Even that brought its own pressures which the public cannot be expected to understand. Just as Charlie Nicholas was being signed up by a big London agent, I was being pursued by the same Bev Walker. These chaps look around for likely prospects and make an offer to manage their public affairs. It had happened in the sixties when Mark McCormack became the agent of great golfers like Jack Nicklaus and was soon a millionaire in his own right. Others have been following the example ever since, some succeeding, some not. The burst of publicity surrounding Charlie Nicholas was due entirely to Bev Walker. You couldn't open a newspaper or magazine or turn on a television without seeing cheerful Charlie involved in some publicity stunt. There is an argument about whether that kind of thing is good for a footballer or not. It certainly wasn't new. In the 1920s Alec Jackson of Aberdeen, one of the Wembley Wizards, had gone to Chelsea and got himself involved in all sorts of advertising stunts in London.

In more recent times, Peter Marinello of Hibs had gone to Arsenal, become the pin-up boy of London and seemed to succeed at everything except football. I'm sure his career didn't shape up the way he had hoped. Now it was Charlie Nicholas's turn and people were arguing as to whether it was a good thing for a young lad to have his head blown up in glossy magazines.

I was five years older than Charlie but Mr Walker wanted to have me in his stable of stars. It is a bewildering situation when you are an innocent wee fellow like me. I had to depend on my instinct. As a schoolboy, you may recall, I resisted the pressures of going to Manchester United because I thought it was more important to prove myself in Scotland first. As a more experienced footballer, I considered the approaches then showed the representatives the door. After all, could you really imagine me dressed up in suede suits and wearing an earring? Wee Gavin would laugh at that. 'No,' I said, 'leave that to Charlie. I'll go my own way.' Maybe I was losing out on a lot of money but I prefer my independence. As I say, these are some of the pressures the public cannot possibly get to know about.

In that run up to the first-leg match in Munich the rest of the boys were playing like demons to win a regular place in the team. Players like Neil Simpson, Doug Bell, Neale Cooper and Mark McGhee were playing out of their skins and Andy Watson was putting pressure on them all to keep on their toes. I had to live with the hope that I would wake up one morning and find there had been some dramatic improvement in the hamstring. The nearer the big night the more I knew I wasn't going to be fully fit.

The boss had a talk with me and asked if I thought I could do a job. He was anxious to present as strong a front to the Germans as possible. I said I would do what I could although I wouldn't be fit for a whole game. Fergie had pulled off a bit of a coup when he returned from his spying trip to Munich with six video films of Bayern in action. We began our homework with three hours of it on the bus journey to Glasgow to play Celtic. Then we all took turns watching the videos at home and they proved a tremendous help to us. It was the small points I found myself picking out. Paul Breitner, for example, never seemed to chase backwards. He simply waited for the ball out of defence then used tremendous speed. I didn't realize he was so fast till I saw that film. Their long crosses were another feature which I was able to study in the comfort of my own armchair. It was all part of our preparation and another sign of how thorough Fergie could be with his homework.

The excitement which had been mounting throughout the Northeast reached a high pitch as we set out for Munich, determined to prove our worth to the Germans whose sides had been knocking us out of Europe in recent years by the odd goal. Those teams had been Fortuna Dusseldorf, Eintracht Frankfurt and more recently Hamburg. Were we ever going to stop this German domination of Aberdeen? Dyce airport was a bustle of activity that March morning as the Pittodrie party arrived for the flight to Munich. Bus loads of supporters were already on their way and the airborne ones were filing through the international departure door as we bought our morning papers, enjoyed our bacon rolls and received the best wishes of everyone around.

The team plane was the fourth to take off for Munich and it was not long before the Bavarian capital was hit by twelve hundred enthusiastic Aberdonians, intent on enjoying themselves whatever the result. It was an especially happy party and Munich was a particularly elegant city. Everything was just right. We drove from the airport to the Sheraton Hotel while the supporters were being delivered to other top-class hotels in the city. They were staying at the Holiday Inn, the Hilton and the Arabella, which was just across the street from the team's hotel. It is not often that players' wives come on foreign trips but Claire Miller, Jill McLeish and Jackie McGhee were there to cheer us on, staying at the Arabella. Once we had checked in we began to explore the hotel and found that Pan's People were dancing there that night and were in the middle of rehearsals. They allowed us to watch but the hotel manager appeared on the scene and asked us to leave. He didn't want anyone to have a free show! So we went off to bed for an afternoon rest before being taken to the stadium at night. Bayern play in the complex built for the Olympic Games of 1972 and the first impression of it was quite breathtaking. The stadium is part of a whole network of tracks and indoor arenas, like a small town in its own right. Oddly enough, as we took in our first sight of the place and later played our match there, I had completely forgotten that it had been the scene of the Israeli massacre during the Olympics. It was only after I was back home and watching a television documentary that the murderous attack on the Israeli athletes came back to me. The stadium looked like Spiderman's house, designed with a web-like effect and with a playing surface which was fantastic.

I had my own warm-up session with the boss who knew I would be on the bench at the start and would come on depending on how the game was going. As usual, I was sharing a room with Stuart Kennedy and we were in bed by eleven o'clock. With two kids rampaging about the house, I'm usually awake by half past seven at home but we lay in until a quarter to nine that morning before going down for breakfast. We had risen to find a morning mist but it soon cleared as we went back to the stadium for an early workout. The Germans apparently expressed some surprise that the boss was insisting on being there on the morning of the match.

'But nobody has ever done this before,' they said.

'Aye,' said Fergie, 'but nobody has ever won here before!'

Local forecasts were saying that Bayern would build up a first-leg margin of 5–0 and even the great Franz Beckenbauer was misguided enough to join in the belittling of Aberdeen. Our own fans were saying we would be doing well to hold them to 2–0, in the hope that we could cancel out that score at Pittodrie.

That afternoon we went back to bed for a rest. Unless you are Willie Miller, who sleeps half his life away, it is difficult to doze off with the excitement of a big match on your mind. Despite his calm on the field and in the

103

dressing room, Doug Bell can't sleep on those occasions.

You are inclined to lie awake and play through the game in advance. Younger players hope they won't make mistakes. You try to make plans for what you will do if the ball comes to you this way or that. Will you shoot or try to chip the goalkeeper? Your mind gets into a bit of a whirl. It is a great help to have people like Fergie and Archie Knox in charge. The boss's reading of a game in advance is quite uncanny. He must work it out in great detail. Archie Knox is a good observer and came up with a detailed dossier of the opposition after he had completed his spying missions. He acquainted us first with the players' names and their peculiarities. It is good to know which foot they use and whether the goalie has a weak side. Archie had all the answers.

On the evening of the match we gathered for our last meeting at five o'clock, a kind of psyching-up session. After tea and toast we were on our way to the stadium. Most players don't like to arrive too early but we could take no chances of a hold-up since the early evening traffic was already streaming out of Munich. We could see the lines of cars, with their lights on, from our hotel window. Once inside the Olympic Stadium we followed the standard procedure of going out to look at the pitch. I don't know why footballers always do that except that it may help decide which studs will suit the conditions. It was a fine crisp, clear night as our twelve hundred supporters streamed into the stands, causing some confusion with their red scarves since Bayern's colours were also red. I was sitting on the bench as the boys set about what was liable to be the toughest test of their lives so far.

You have to put reputations out of your mind and get on with your own game – and that is what Aberdeen did in Munich that night. They gave a display of concentration which was absolutely fantastic and non-stop concentration is the key to any success you can hope to have over a team of that calibre. The Germans play a lot of one-two football and if you take your mind off the game for a second they will punish you without mercy. The secret is to make sure the man who makes the first pass doesn't get the return he is expecting. Our lads excelled at it. Willie Miller blotted out the great Rummenigge. Neale Cooper kept close to Breitner. And for my money the best man on the park was Doug Bell. The longer the game went without a German goal, the better Aberdeen became. At half-time you calculate that your opponents have lost forty-five minutes of their chances to score and that gives you great heart to renew your efforts in the second half. And so it went. Aberdeen took more and more command of the game and found they had nothing to fear from these great names of German football. The boss had me out on the touchline warming up, then told me to get my tracksuit off. With just fifteen minutes left, I went on to replace Eric Black. Even though I was not fully fit, he saw it as a good psychological move. The Germans knew my name from the World Cup and the idea that I might turn on some of that form was not going to improve their morale. In fact my leg was still far from right and all I did was play into the pattern of the previous seventy-five minutes. When that final whistle blew we knew that, by holding Bayern Munich to a no-scoring draw, we had gained a great moral victory. The fans were tremendous that night. Outnumbered by Germans at the rate of 30–1, they still managed to out-shout them and to send the vibrations of a great night back to Scotland through radio and television.

The boss was delighted without getting too carried away by the draw. The reaction of most people would have been that the toughest part of the tie was behind us and that, if we managed to hold them in Germany, we would surely complete the job on our own ground. Straightaway, Fergie took the opposite view and of course he was right again. With a great record of success at home, Bayern were also past masters at drawing their away games. A scoring draw at Pittodrie was all they would need to put them through to the semifinal on the away-goal rule. And who would say they were unlikely to make it 1–1 or 2–2? It is the kind of neat situation that great teams manage to engineer for themselves. On the domestic level, Rangers used to be good at it. As Fergie made clear, any relaxation on our part and Bayern would kill us off at Pittodrie.

17

Pittodrie's Greatest Night

That night in Munich was one for quiet celebration and
the fans felt the same way. They came to our hotel and
behaved in exemplary fashion. Because there wasn't a
hooligan element about, they were able to drink in the
large cocktail area of the Sheraton Hotel where the
players were also enjoying a glass of beer. They enjoyed a
chat with the boys who were ready as ever to sign
autographs and have a word with these people who had
gone to the trouble and expense of travelling all that way
to cheer us on. Their contribution that night had been a
tremendous boost to the lads on the field and you could
sense that the fans themselves were aware that they had
played their part in a great achievement. Some supporters had been phoning home and were bringing back
news that everybody had been hanging on every word of
the commentaries of the BBC and North Sound and the
whole Northeast was in raptures. Next morning we set
out for home very contented with our result but remembering the boss's warning about keeping our feet on the
ground and not falling for the old Scottish weakness of
thinking we are the greatest before collapsing with a
thud.

It had been an exhausting night and we would
welcome an early bed on the Thursday before setting out
again on the Friday for an away league fixture at
Kilmarnock. That was why we were less than pleased
with twenty-seven firemen at Aberdeen airport who
decided to stage a strike over some grievance or other

just as we were due back.

No planes can land while firemen are not on duty but what angered us was that they allowed the first three loads of supporters to come down then staged their strike which stopped the team plane from landing. If that was their idea of getting publicity for their cause it wasn't very clever. How much better publicity they would have got if they had lifted their ban. With friends and fans waiting at the airport, it would have seemed like a generous gesture to a team which had just done Aberdeen proud. With the other planes safely down at Dyce, we were diverted to Edinburgh to await buses for another three-hour journey north. I don't know if I'm psychic but we had no sooner settled into our coach for Aberdeen when I made a rather cynical remark to some of the lads.

'All we need is for this bus to break down,' I said.

The words were no sooner out than smoke began to belch from under the bus – and we were stuck again. As I say, the firemen at Aberdeen airport were not our favourite people that day.

When we finally made it home, the fever was already building up for the return match in two weeks' time. Tickets were snapped up to the full Pittodrie capacity of around 25,000 and I found myself having phone calls from people I had forgotten, asking about my health and my wife and kids and then, as an afterthought, wondering if there were any tickets to be had.

I still wasn't fully fit but nothing was going to stop me from being on the field that night. The build-up of excitement in the city was unbelievable as the Bayern team flew into Aberdeen and settled in at the Skean Dhu Hotel at Altens.

Here we were, about to entertain one of the greatest clubs in the world and the prize for beating them over this one game was a place in the semifinal of the European Cup Winners' Cup. What a prospect!

All Pittodrie was buzzing as the game kicked off and we forced three corners in the first five minutes. We were putting Bayern under tremendous pressure. With all their experience, however, they weathered the storm and got out of their difficulties in the best possible way. They scored. Alec McLeish clashed with Hoeness and the French referee gave a free kick to Bayern, which we disputed. With the side of his foot, Paul Breitner tapped the ball to Augenthaler, who veered further to the right and released a shot which went streaking into the net, touching Jim Leighton's hand on the way. I had a run at the Bayern goal in an attempt to get back on level terms but the Germans kept up their pressure and Rummenigge sent the tricky little Del'Haye away on a dangerous run. Aberdeen were by no means out of it, with Eric Black heading against the crossbar and Peter Weir and Neale Cooper coming close to scoring. We were building up to an equalizer. In thirty-eight minutes Mark McGhee judged his cross perfectly, beat the keeper and found Eric Black, whose header was blocked by Augenthaler, the man who had scored their goal. With typical grit, Neil Simpson came dashing in from nowhere and forced the ball home, while the big defender made a second attempt to clear it. We were at least on equal terms again but, if nothing else happened, the Germans would go through on the 1–1 score.

That possibility grew stronger in the sixteenth minute of the second half when Del'Haye and Dremmler combined well on the right. The full back's cross was back-headed by Hoeness and in came Pflugler to send a tremendous left-foot shot swerving past Jim Leighton. The boss was not long in reacting. He sent on John McMaster for Stuart Kennedy, moving Doug Rougvie to left back, Neale Cooper to right back, with John taking over in midfield.

At 2–1 down, the fans went incredibly quiet, feeling pessimistically that it was all over. Some of the younger lads in the team were also lowering their heads and feeling a bit bewildered by what was going on. But some of the older heads were taking a different attitude and telling the younger ones to keep going. It wasn't all over.

It is not a case of being wise after the event but, even with fifteen minutes left for play, I had a real feeling that something was going to happen. What's more, despite our desperate need for those two goals, I found myself thoroughly enjoying the game. I knew in my own mind it wasn't all over.

John Hewitt had just come on for Neil Simpson when things began to happen. Fifteen minutes left. I was fouled to the right of the German penalty box at the King Street end. As we placed the ball for the free kick, John McMaster and I remembered that, even though our double-act was well-known to Scottish football, the Germans had probably never heard of it. There are still people, incidentally, who think we are genuinely getting in each other's way. The scene was set. Big Alec McLeish got the message and ran up to his spot in the penalty area.

John and I started our run, bumped together, pretended to blame each other then turned away as if in disarray. That is the point when our opponents relax, thinking we will take time to regroup. That's the moment when I turned quickly, apparently without looking where I was putting the ball, and chipped it to the spot where Alec McLeish was stationed. We had practised it dozens of times. With Bayern's defence still wondering what was happening, big Alec rose like a bird and angled his header well out of Muller's reach. 2–2! Pittodrie went daft. If the supporters had been depressed before, they now sensed that something could still happen after all. If I had a feeling that something was in the air before, I knew it now for certain. The tide was flowing for us. I didn't have time to think too much about it before the next sensation came along. The television cameras were still lingering on Alec McLeish, the scorer, when they found themselves almost missing the greatest drama of all. That magnificent placer of a ball, John McMaster, gained possession straight from Bayern's restart, moved forward a few paces and sent a high ball to reach Eric Black's head with perfection. Eric rose and guided the

110

ball to Muller's right-hand side. The keeper dived and did well to palm the ball downwards. And who was on the spot but the man they had come to call Super Sub himself – John Hewitt. Some people have said the ball just hit him accidentally but there was more to it than that. John angled himself from a very difficult position, brought the bouncing ball down very skilfully and put it right through the keeper's legs as he struggled to recover from his previous dive. From 2–1 down, ninety seconds ago, we were now 3–2 ahead. Pittodrie couldn't believe it. If this was not the greatest display of football ever produced by the Dons it was certainly the most dramatic moment the Aberdeen ground had ever seen.

Fourteen minutes still to go. Could we hold on to our lead? Bayern would need only to equalize and they would go sailing through to the semifinal. From then on, however, we were in control of the game. Surprisingly, our fitness turned out to be far superior to theirs. I was full of running right to the final whistle and I couldn't see Bayern scoring. When Rummenigge showed a flash of danger Willie Miller came along and brushed him aside with his usual efficiency.

As the minutes ticked away the crowd built up their own sound, which exploded in celebration when the referee blew that whistle. Yes, we had beaten the great Bayern Munich and gained ourselves a famous victory which would take us to a position many people didn't believe was possible. The semifinal of the European Cup Winners' Cup. The supporters were rejoicing over a memorable victory while I was trying to take it all in quietly. Nobody wanted to leave Pittodrie that night and little wonder. When you came to analyse it, the genius of Fergie's substitutions stood out as the main factor. The cool head of John McMaster coming on to put away those telling crosses. Then John Hewitt with his amazing knack of arriving at vital moments and snatching winners. Yes, the boss had triumphed again. And there he was, skipping down the tunnel like a five-year-old and into the dressing room where pandemonium was breaking loose. If it was time for quiet enjoyment in Munich two weeks earlier, it was time for some noisy celebration this time. It had proved to be the harder part of the tie, as Fergie warned us, but we had come through it with flying colours.

18

Gothenburg, Here We Come!

On the morning after Pittodrie's greatest night, the supporters were already thinking about the final. But Gothenburg was not entering my head at that point. There was still a semifinal to get through and when the draw was made we found ourselves paired with what seemed the least-fancied team, Waterschei of Belgium. But we discovered that they had a remarkable home record of not being beaten in something like three years. We knew no more about them than they probably knew about us so there was a chance that they were a team on our own level. Certainly no team was going to reach the semifinal of a European competition without having something to offer.

The Belgians arrived in Aberdeen for the first leg and once again Pittodrie was packed out for the floodlit occasion. The game had the most sensational start when Dougie Bell embarked on perhaps his greatest-ever run, went right through the Waterschei defence and sent an angled ball towards the far post. Eric Black was running up in time to put us into the lead in the first minute of the game. Dougie Bell, the quiet man of Pittodrie, becomes quieter still when asked if he was really passing the ball to Eric or trying a shot at goal himself! We gave him the benefit of the doubt that he really did mean to pass it. But if that was a sensational start, there was more to come. Before Waterschei could gather themselves, the loon from Newmachar, Neil Simpson himself, had challenged for the ball and proceeded to survive three tackles before hammering home a second goal.

Pittodrie awaited a goal feast but it wasn't going to be as easy as that. In fact, if we had not knocked Waterschei off their stride with those two goals, I believe anything could have happened. We had a sticky spell after that. I was getting some barracking from the crowd who hadn't forgotten that I missed an important penalty against St Mirren on the previous Saturday when goals and points were vital if we were to have any chance of the league title. Into the second half, Mark McGhee guided home a ball after more relentless work by Dougie Bell. Waterschei had pulled one back before Peter Weir made it 4–1 with a header at the left-hand post and Mark completed the score at 5–1 with a goal which looked as if it was never going to happen! I was right through when I squared the ball to Mark, who had the first try at goal. It was stopped on the line before Mark and Willie Miller and Mark again tried to force it over the line. He was on the ground when he finally scooped it in, with a brave defender lying in the goalmouth having done everything possible to keep it out. I felt a bit sorry for him.

At 5–1 there were not many people doubting that we would be appearing in the European Cup Winners' Cup Final in Gothenburg. Most folk were digging out their atlases to find exactly where Gothenburg was. Harry Hinds, the club's official travel agent in Glasgow, was already booking his planes and making arrangements because there would not be a great deal of time to make plans for all those thousands who intended to travel. Little else was being spoken about in the Northeast. A return match had still to be played in Belgium but not many fans were planning to go there, since the journey to Gothenburg was going to stretch many a bank account. Before Belgium, however, we had by now reached the semifinal of the Scottish Cup and were due to play Celtic at Hampden Park on the Saturday before leaving for the Continent on the Monday. That turned out to be a real bruiser of a game, the roughest Aberdeen–Celtic match I have ever known. Celtic were still battling for the league title with Dundee United and ourselves, a battle which they were eventually to lose. The Scottish Cup was vital to their pride and honour for Celtic were not in the habit of failing in both the major competitions. It was billed as the 'final in advance' but it was a poor advertisement for a final or any other kind of football match, by my reckoning. I was effectively out of action within fifteen minutes with a twisted knee and ankle, but I played on, though I was quite unable to use the outside of my foot. Eric Black was crocked and Dougie Bell received a really bad injury, which was to have disastrous repercussions for him. On top of all that, Neale Cooper was injured twice and long before the final whistle was lying in the Victoria Infirmary, near Hampden Park, with his nose coming out at the back of his head. At first he was concussed and seemed to be wandering about in a daze. I tried to check how bad he was and asked him some questions.

'I can see two ball boys,' he told me.

'That's OK, Neale,' I said. 'There *are* two ball boys!'

But the lad was in a bad way all right and was soon on his way to hospital. I teased him that it was time he had something like a broken nose. He's far too good looking anyway. We were a sorry looking lot as we left Hampden that Saturday teatime, wondering what kind of team would be available to face Waterschei on the Tuesday.

Was this the kind of thing that could happen to us? Playing with half a team, would this be the occasion when Waterschei would make a tremendous run at us and cancel out our four-goal advantage? On the bus going back to Aberdeen we at least had the consolation that Peter Weir had scored the only goal of the game against Celtic and we were through to another Scottish Cup Final, when we would meet Rangers for the second year running. But that was away in the future and it was surely a sign of the times at Aberdeen that we were not even thinking about that occasion yet. There were more important things on hand.

We went to Belgium two days later with a sorely depleted team and were beaten 1–0, which still put us

115

through to the final on an aggregate of 5–2. Most people would have been turning cartwheels at that but you would have thought there was a disaster in the Dons' dressing room afterwards. What annoyed the lads was that we had come all this way without a single defeat in any of the legs. We badly wanted to keep that record intact but with so many casualties around it was maybe asking too much. The match was at least memorable for young Willie Falconer, the lanky forward who made his European debut that night at the age of sixteen. That will be something to tell his grandchildren about. As for the rest of us, the heads were down. When Harry Hinds, the travel agent, came bursting into the dressing room, he was ready to lead a celebration with a bottle of champagne. But Harry's enthusiasm was soon quietened by the mood of the lads who were so disappointed about the defeat. It was early to bed that night and the morning put a better complexion on things when we put it all behind us and realized that we could now say without any fear at all, 'Gothenburg, here we come!'

The big blackspot that night, apart from the fact that Dougie Bell was already out of action, was a serious injury to Mister Fitness himself, Stuart Kennedy, who rarely missed a game but looked in danger of being out for some time.

We were still deeply involved in three contests – through to the finals of the Scottish Cup and the European Cup Winners' Cup and in contention for the Premier League title. But whatever impression was being given to the public, there was no doubt about the priority in the minds of the players. That European trophy was our No.1 aim. The week before Gothenburg our Saturday match with Kilmarnock was brought forward to the Thursday to give us a longer break before the big night. Pittodrie was packed for that league game with Killie. It was a last chance for those fans who were not going to the final to give us a send-off – and that was what they did. They were putting some cheers into our ears that we would carry with us to Sweden and luckily we gave them something to cheer about, beating Kilmarnock 5–0. I scored two.

We came off the park that night knowing that the next time we would trot out as a team it would be on the biggest occasion in the history of Aberdeen Football Club. It was the sole topic of conversation wherever we went. On the Saturday, I went down to see my old pal George Mackie playing for Brechin City against my local team in Edinburgh, Meadowbank – the two top teams in the Second Division, about to win promotion to the First. Everybody was wishing me all the best for the following week and making me realize how much we were playing for Scotland and not just for Aberdeen.

Sunday was a quiet day at home before the big trek to Sweden began the following day. My sister Laura, who came to visit us in Aberdeen and stayed on to find herself a job and a boyfriend in the city, was on her way across the North Sea on the St Clair. We were up bright and early that Monday morning and Lesley drove me to Pittodrie where the bus would collect us all and take us to the airport. Lesley doesn't enjoy flying but this was an occasion she couldn't miss and she was due to fly out with the wives on the following day.

It has become a bit of a superstition that we must have our bacon rolls and sausage rolls at the airport before we board a plane so this was no time to break the custom. The first of the supporters' planes was already taking off and they would be followed by many more on the Tuesday and even on the Wednesday morning until there would be around 12,000 Aberdeen fans in Gothenburg.

It was surprising how many were actually making the journey by bus and car, travelling all the way down to the south of England, crossing on ferries to Holland and France and carrying on through Germany and Denmark before crossing on another ferry to Sweden.

Our plane took off smoothly, out across the North Sea, and in no time at all we were preparing to land in Gothenburg. Most of the fans were booked at hotels

117

inside the city but they waited to see us through as we boarded a coach for the hotel at Farshatt, about fifteen miles outside the city. The name of the hotel gave rise to a lot of Aberdeenshire banter when people asked what it was called. 'Farshatt,' we said. To which they were liable to ask again, 'Far's 'at?' It was situated in a nice wee village with a river running through it, the kind of quiet place you need when there are a lot of fans around. Don't get me wrong. We love to see our fans but if they come chanting around your hotel on a big occasion like that you can become a bit edgy and maybe say things you don't really mean. There are some supporters who follow us faithfully on some of our foreign trips when there is only the team plane travelling. These same people have the privilege of being with us on the bigger occasions when there are other planes besides our own. They were even allowed to stay in our hotel at Farshatt.

On the first night we had a team meeting at which every detail of Real Madrid was examined. Archie Knox had completed his dossier once again, though with a great deal more difficulty this time.

On his main mission to study their play he found himself let down on the promise that there would be a ticket waiting for him at the ground. He was near to missing the game when, according to the story, he had to employ a bit of bribery to get inside! All that didn't stop Archie from doing his usual excellent job, giving us valuable pointers on what to expect from different players. Some of us older ones join in on these discussions to clarify anything we are not sure about.

While the hotel itself was excellent, we did run into a snag with the size of the rooms. They were too small and the beds looked as if they had been designed for the Seven Dwarfs. So we were smartly moved to an annexe where everything was to our satisfaction. On the Tuesday afternoon, as the fans continued to pour into the city, we drove to the Ullevi stadium for a full-scale work-out. It was a warm, sunny day, giving us a totally false impression of what it would be like on the night.

Workmen were still putting last-minute touches to the stadium as we trotted out for our training session. The Press and television cameras were there and a number of fans had managed to find their way on to the terracing. People like Ian St John, Brian Moore and Hugh McIlvanney were strolling around the park and the photographers were being given every facility to take our pictures. Fergie had invited Jock Stein to come along with our party and that was another astute move on the part of the boss. The fact that the international manager is in your camp adds an extra dimension, especially to the younger players, who would want to impress him with their conduct as well as their play.

Mr Stein was no doubt a great help to Fergie, still a young man in managerial terms and able to draw, if necessary, on the experience of the former Celtic boss who had been through all this before.

It was a pleasant afternoon out there in the Ullevi stadium and I tried to take a good look around and to wonder what it would all be like on the night. Once the photographers had had their allotted time, the boss cleared the field and we played a short, sharp game of football, across the park instead of up and down it. We had been allocated an hour for our training session and Real Madrid had the hour after that. Maybe the boss was learning about psychological warfare but we were in no hurry to come off the park at the end of our time! The Real players were standing in the tunnel awaiting their turn. That was the first we had seen of them. As we trotted off, they trotted on, but there was no contact between us. We went off back to our hotel with only one slight nagging doubt in my mind about the Ullevi stadium. The grass was too long. I didn't know if they intended to cut it before the game but, if it stayed the length it was then, I felt it was going to be to Real's advantage. I didn't know there was going to be a change in the weather.

Back at the hotel we settled down to our last evening before the big game. It could have been a difficult night but we all relaxed with a meal followed by a quiz, chaired by Alan Ferguson of Proscot, the company which organized the commercial side of the players' involvement in Europe, including our recording of the 'European Song'. For the quiz we were divided into seven teams of three and the trio of Archie Knox, Bryan Gunn and myself ended up as winners.

As I have said, everyone has the greatest regard for Teddy Scott but an incident during that quiz produced the only flash of anger I've ever seen to cross his face. He was asked to write down the name of a football team with nineteen letters. He got the correct answer – Hamilton Academicals – but he misspelled it and lost the points! For once, our Ted was ruffled. Maybe the pressures were getting to him as well.

After the quiz we were off to bed, trying to get as good a sleep as possible before the great day.

19

The Heavens Open

On the morning of 11 May we were out of our beds in good time, ready for a session at the training ground of the Swedish national team. Everybody was on edge. You could sense it all round. If anybody had said a word out of place they were liable to get a punch on the nose. Of all the players, the occasion was getting to Peter Weir most of all. By his reaction to one of the boss's remarks I knew he was not behaving normally. Thoroughbreds are like that. And who could blame him? He wanted to play the match there and then. We all wanted to play the match there and then. But there was all afternoon between us and the evening.

When it started to rain around lunchtime we were not at all worried because we like some rain on the pitch. On the previous afternoon there had even been some talk that it was possibly too dry. Then it was off to bed for the afternoon lie-down, whether you managed to sleep or not. When we rose at half past four the weather situation was more worrying, with the skies black and ugly and the rain coming down quite heavily. Mark McGhee was up before most of us and was trying to soothe himself at the pin-ball machine. A man cracked a joke about him missing an easy one on the machine – just as he had done in a match the previous week! Mark nearly hit him. That was how tense the whole situation had become.

So we sat down to our light meal, in my case the usual poached egg on toast, and began to count the minutes till we left the hotel. Some supporters were milling around, wishing us all the best and finally we stepped on to the bus and took our usual seats – John McMaster, Alec McLeish, Stuart Kennedy and I (poor Stuart had not recovered from the Waterschei injury though he was being given a seat on the bench) sitting at the back of the bus where we normally have our card school. This time, on the journey from Farshatt to the Ullevi Stadium, I was wearing my Sony Walkman headset and listening to music, cutting myself off from the atmosphere of the bus. It was also helping to divert me from the worrying situation of the weather. Lightning was flashing all around us and nobody is too keen to run about when lightning is liable to catch up with you. I was listening to the music, thinking about the length of that grass and watching the flashes in the sky. It was all very dramatic, as if there wasn't enough drama surrounding the occasion already.

When we arrived at Ullevi about an hour and a quarter before kick-off, I jumped for joy to see that they had tarpaulins on the grass and that, however much the pitch might cut up afterwards, at least we would be starting with reasonable conditions. What would have happened if they had not taken the precaution of covering the pitch could be seen by the atrocious conditions behind the goal areas. I doubt if we could possibly have played. We couldn't venture too far out to inspect the surface since the rain was still teeming down. By now they were beginning to haul the tarpaulins away.

Even by stepping out to the track we were in danger of being soaked. That would come soon enough. When I returned to the dressing room my hair was dripping down over my eyes. In one of those crazy scenes at a vital moment, the boss wanted to cut my hair but I insisted on taking the scissors and cutting it myself. So that is the last thing I did in the minutes before the European Cup Winners' Cup Final – gave myself a do-it-yourself haircut! It looked a fair old mess in the morning but who was caring in the morning?

In strange surroundings, we changed into our familiar

strip and realized that the great moment was ever so near now. An unusual hush descended on the dressing room as everyone went into his own thoughts, maybe his own prayers, and we just sat looking at each other. It was not until five minutes before we were due to take the field that reality returned. That was the moment when we all started screaming and shouting, like a bunch of schoolboys. It is part of the necessary psyching-up for a big occasion. Alec McLeish is always shouting. The lads began to shake hands and wish each other all the best. My style is to tell the boys to enjoy themselves above all else. I looked at the lads, Neale Cooper, Neil Simpson, Eric Black and John Hewitt, and wondered what was going through their young minds. They were showing no nerves but it must have been affecting them on the inside. The boss gave us his final words. All the planning was over now, he said. It was up to us, out there in the Ullevi Stadium of Gothenburg.

Suddenly a bell rang and that was our signal to leave the dressing room. Out we trooped to line up for a few minutes in the tunnel and that was a curious experience. For we were standing just an arm's length away from the Real Madrid team, across the passage, side by side, casting an odd glance at each other but never exchanging as much as a smile. This was time for serious battle. No time to be fraternizing with the enemy. Standing for those few minutes, our lads were on such a high of emotion that they wanted to start playing the game there in the tunnel.

Out in the stands and terracings the crowd was well below what should have been witnessing a European final but that is so often the situation on those occasions, so far removed from the countries involved. From the players' point of view, however, you could have fooled us about the empty gaps. As we finally walked out, side by side with Real under those Ullevi floodlights, the surrounding area was pitch black as far as our vision was concerned. But we could hear those 12,000 Aberdonians and believe me, they sounded as if they were filling every inch of that stadium. So for us there was no lack of atmosphere. The rain still teemed down as the formalities ended and we lined up for the biggest event of our lives. Apart from having it video-taped, there will not be many Aberdeen supporters who will not remember every detail of that incredible game for the rest of their lives.

The Scottish players crowd round after the World Cup goal in Sweden

I tangle with three Brazilian players in the 1982 World Cup

Above left: The Scottish sports photographers chose me as 1982 Sports Personality of the Year, following in the footsteps of Jim Watt, Sandy Lyle, John Greig, Allan Wells and Andy Irvine

Above right: Christmas time with Lesley and the kids, Craig and Gavin

Below left: Tom Gemmell in his playing days for Celtic. Later he was my manager at Dundee

Below right: Jimmy Johnstone also spent a short but memorable time at Dundee

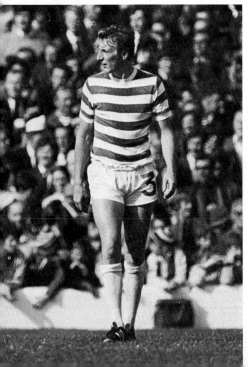

The Ullevi Stadium, Gothenburg, where it all happened

A clever touch from fans at the Dons-Bayern Munich match, quarterfinal of the European Cup Winners' Cup, 1983

GORDONSTRACHAN!

Eric Black scores the first goal against Real Madrid in the European Cup Winners' Cup Final, 1983, in Gothenburg

John Hewitt's famous goal which capped Pittodrie's greatest night and made it 3-2 for Aberdeen against Bayern Munich, 1983

20

Our VE Night

In conditions which were far from suitable for good football, we dived straight into the game and Eric Black gave warning of our danger when he struck the crossbar. Real didn't expect that so soon. In just seven minutes we gave them something else to ponder over at siesta time. I took a corner on the right and up came big Alec McLeish, just as we had planned, to head the ball forcibly towards goal. It was blocked near the line and that was when Eric Black wheeled round in classical fashion and drove the ball into the net. One up! What a boost to the team. The fans could hardly take it in. Nor could they take in the disaster which followed soon after. Poor Alec McLeish. In an unusual lapse of concentration he made that pass-back to Jim Leighton and didn't allow for the heavy ground. The ball stuck in the water and Santillana was on it like a flash, streaking across the penalty area as Jim Leighton came out in a desperate bid to avert a score. It was almost inevitable that he was going to bring down the Spanish player. A penalty. Juanito scored and we had lost the advantage we so richly deserved. They then began to run the game and it was not until ten minutes before half-time that we gathered ourselves and started coming back into it again.

By half-time we had had our fright and the boss was telling us in the dressing room, 'We're right back into the game, lads.' He also told me to take a breather in the early part of the second half so that I wouldn't run myself into the ground. No doubt he was thinking about the possibility of extra time and the fact that I would need to have some wind left to run at Real when energy might be sagging and concentration slipping.

Aberdeen started well in the second half, just as we had done in the first, and I was soon forgetting the boss's instructions to take it easy. I couldn't hold back and found myself going forward, looking for possession, taking on men, trying to chip the goalkeeper and having one particular shot which the keeper saved with his foot. Peter Weir was coming more and more into the game and who will ever forget that remarkable run down the wing when he hurdled over four Real challenges like a steeplechaser and sent over an inviting cross for Eric Black. It seemed like a simple opportunity which he headed over the bar and the crowd thought he could have done better. Actually that ball had such a wild spin on it I didn't think Eric had a chance of directing it properly. With three minutes of normal time to go, Eric limped off to be replaced by John Hewitt, the man who had a remarkable knack of pulling us through at vital moments.

When full-time came and the score remained at 1–1, as it had done since the fourteenth minute of the match, we faced thirty minutes of extra time and, worse than that, the chance that this great occasion might be decided by penalty kicks, at which the Spaniards were supposed to be better than us.

In extra time we made a claim for a penalty when Neale Cooper seemed to be fouled and had an even stronger claim when Mark McGhee was felled. Into the second period of extra time, with just fifteen minutes between us and a penalty decider, we tried everything we knew to win the game with football.

What happened next is history. Peter Weir drew three players around him near the dugout, beat two of them and chipped a splendid ball to Mark McGhee down the left wing. Mark did magnificently well to get round his marker and cross with his left foot. The keeper, diving out to intercept, misjudged it by inches and there was you-know-who, John Hewitt himself, launching his body on that dive which put his own name as well as that of Aberdeen and Scottish football into the record books.

With eight minutes to go, that ball was in the back of the net. John was dancing a Highland Fling and the whole Ullevi Stadium erupted with delight. What a moment! But there were still those minutes to go. The cup was not yet won and Real Madrid were always capable of pulling off something spectacular.

The only real danger came with just two minutes to go, when they were awarded that free kick just outside our penalty box. Would they manage one of those raking shots that continental teams can so often produce out of the blue? They took the kick but it was blocked. Then, to our consternation, the referee decided to give them a second chance, apparently on the grounds that they had taken it before he had blown his whistle. I don't know about that but I do know what was happening when they lined up for their second chance – the one that might just deprive us of our famous victory.

As the Aberdeen players lined up their wall and tried to cover as much of our goal as possible, I was suddenly aware of a voice behind me. Somebody was earnestly saying a prayer.

'Please, God,' the voice was saying, 'don't let them score. They don't deserve it!'

It was Peter Weir, the man who had done so much to make this victory possible and was now bringing in the Lord to help out in this last-ditch attempt to prevent an equalizer. Well, Peter's prayer worked, as we all know. The ball went streaking past by about a foot. Jim Leighton heaved a sigh of relief and only had time to place his goal-kick and belt it downfield when the greatest sound of all came blasting into our ears. It was all over. Aberdeen had won the European Cup Winners' Cup and the Ullevi Stadium was going daft.

The players were jumping about, shaking hands, slapping backs, congratulating each other. The boss

127

came out of the dugout like a man possessed, fell into a puddle and Archie Knox ran right over him on his way to the players. Willie Miller couldn't wait to get his hands on that cup and, when he did, we set off round the park to greet those fans who had given us such wonderful support from first minute to last. Big Doug Rougvie was going haywire. John McMaster was poising the cup on his head. How well these two had performed at full back, never putting a foot out of place all evening.

Stuart Kennedy joined in the celebration, though he and Dougie Bell had had the heartbreaking experience of not being on the park on that greatest of occasions. I went to congratulate Stuart for his part in getting us there but I knew there was nothing that could possibly console him for not being in at the death. He had been so fit all these years, so free of injury, and then fate dealt him this cruel blow when it all mattered. He could hardly bring himself to touch the cup. I was sorry for Andy Watson and so sorry for Dougie Bell, who had played such a magnificent part in those earlier rounds. Who would forget Dougie's dominance in that crucial game in Munich when he was the best man on the park? Who would forget his rip-roaring start against Waterschei in the semifinal when he set Pittodrie alight, taking on the whole defence himself in that opening minute and setting us on course for what might otherwise have been a very difficult road to the final?

Poor Doug wasn't even going to get a medal. It is worth recording that Andy Watson, who received a medal as a substitute, made a very genuine offer to Doug to accept his one but the quiet man of Pittodrie thanked him for his kindness and refused. The medal position strikes me as an unsatisfactory one though I can see the difficulty in changing it. When people like Stuart Kennedy and Doug Bell make such a contribution to an achievement like that, there should be some way of rewarding them. I take nothing away from young lads like Bryan Gunn and Ian Angus, who were on the bench that night and therefore received their medals. But they would be the first to agree that they made virtually no contribution to the victory and were less deserving of the award.

In the midst of that victory celebration I said to Stuart Kennedy, 'I'm sorry I can't help you, Stuart.'

'It's all right, Gordon,' he said. 'Just you enjoy yourself.'

Football is a tough business, without any room for the faint-hearted, but players have feelings as deep as anybody else and it is in moments like that that you realize how human they are.

Now we're back to where this book began: at the height of that greatest moment in our lives my own reaction was not so much to dance around as to just stand there and try to take it all in. This might never happen again in my whole career. The celebrations would go on into the night and be recalled for the rest of our lives. But here we were in the Ullevi Stadium, in the actual moment itself and I was trying to remember as many details as I could. One final round of the perimeter wall, thanking the fans, waving to them, accepting their congratulations, and we were off inside to meet more people and shake more hands, to be interviewed by Archie Macpherson and so on.

Johnny Metgod of Real had asked me to swop strips and he was waiting for me as I returned to the dressing room area. The Real players were hanging around looking pretty downcast. Willie Miller and I were taken away for the routine dope test and were given a couple of beers to assist with the urine sample. We were in the same room as the Real pair and one of them was trying to pee and complain about Mark McGhee's elbows at the same time!

Some of our lads attended a reception at the stadium, along with club officials, but Willie and I missed out on that. We were ready now to return to Farshatt for the club's own celebration, where we would meet up with our wives for the first time in Sweden. They had spent the Tuesday night at the Europa Hotel, which had been the nerve centre of all the supporter activity in Gothenburg, but now they were moving out to spend the Wednesday night with us at the team headquarters. When our coach arrived back at the hotel I made straight for our room, where Lesley was changing to go down to the reception.

Let's just say we had quite an emotional reunion as I burst into the room. Down in the foyer, crowds had waited to greet us, including Swedes who were enjoying a dinner-dance in the hotel. Now we were having drinks in our own reception area before filing through to the buffet-room. It was a very happy celebration night. The directors who had done so much to build this club were there with their wives – Mr Donald and his son Ian, and Mr Anderson. Fergie and Archie and all the lads and their wives or sweethearts were sampling the bubbly stuff. There were speeches and presentations and the boss paid tribute to the long-suffering wives. Jock Stein was there and so was Ernie Walker, secretary of the SFA. Then we went out to the bigger lounge-cum-dancefloor area and continued to enjoy ourselves until far into the night. No doubt with one eye on my bonus, my bank manager, David Hamilton, was there and another friend, Kenny Taylor. It was one of those nights when nobody will be ashamed to say they were tipsy. I was in such an inebriated mood that I finally gave Lesley a piggyback to our room about four o'clock in the morning. Not being a heavy drinker, I was feeling none too clever at breakfast time but my splitting head began to ease off after I jumped into the open-air swimming pool. It was pouring with rain, but who cared?

The wives left before us for the airport to catch an earlier plane to Aberdeen. Then we set out for home, arriving at Gothenburg airport to the cheers of departing fans, who were milling about in their thousands.

On the plane home, the European Cup Winners' Cup was filled with champagne and passed along the aisle for anyone to drink. The players themselves had had enough of the sparkling stuff, remembering that there was still a vital league game to be played against Hibs at Pittodrie in two days' time.

21

What a Welcome!

If we thought we had seen most of the celebrations in Gothenburg, we didn't know the half of what was about to hit us in Aberdeen. Dyce airport itself was a seething mass of returning fans, joined by hundreds more who had come to see us home.

Then we started out on the long journey to Pittodrie which was without doubt one of the most amazing experiences of a lifetime. From the road out of the airport, there was not a vacant space for the rest of our journey. At first it was just cars, parked at the roadside with their occupants out to wave their freshly made banners and cheer us on. At Bucksburn the main street was so solidly packed with people that the bus could hardly move. On we went to Anderson Drive, Queen's Road, Albyn Place, deep with rows of people all the way. When we came to Holburn Junction and realized that Union Street was jam-packed for its whole length, I knew I had never seen anything like this in my life. Even those amazing welcomes to Liverpool we had all seen on television didn't seem to compare with this. The flags, the banners, the splashes of red and white and our bus nosing its way through tens of thousands sent the blood tingling in your veins.

Mind you, we needed some warmth for it was freezing cold on top of that open bus but it was worth every minute of the two hours which it took from Dyce to Pittodrie.

King Street was another sea of faces and flags and

Pittodrie itself was already packed with people who had been there for three hours to welcome us back to our real football home. So there we were, back where it all started nine months earlier when we beat Sion of Switzerland. Who would have believed that we would take on the might of the Continent, with some of the greatest of all football club names between us and victory, and win right through to become the cup champions of Europe? What's more, we had done it without any world-class stars imported from other countries but with a bunch of home-grown lads – four of them from the North and Northeast – most of whom had cost the club nothing but the ability to spot the talent and sign them on.

Needless to say, all this was the high point of my life and when the Pittodrie welcome was over, it was a relaxing change to go home to my house in Albury Road for a cup of tea and a quiet evening.

For our last league game against Hibs on the Saturday, Pittodrie was again filled, partly because there was still a slim chance that we could win the league championship that day but more, I felt, as another chance to pick up the cheering of Gothenburg and give it another belt. So they did – and we were still on Cloud Nine as we proceeded to give Hibs a thorough beating, after they had courteously lined up to applaud us on to the field.

As things turned out that day, Dundee United managed to win and clinch their first-ever league championship so our final effort was in vain. But it had been a great season all round, with a nail-biting finish right to the last kick of the last league game. For once, the main honours in Scotland were bound for neither Ibrox Park nor Parkhead. But, if we were still feeling high during that game with Hibs, the reaction of Gothenburg was not far away.

22

Fergie Fines Me £250

The week that followed Gothenburg remains a big blank in my memory. I do remember talking to the man at the garage on the following Thursday and all he was interested in was Gothenburg. It was the same everywhere. You would never have imagined that on the following Saturday we were due to meet Rangers in the Scottish Cup Final. All things are relative, they say, and it just showed how far along the road of football progress Aberdeen had come. In previous years, when would a cup final with Rangers have been a matter to raise little excitement among the fans and, if the truth be told, among the Dons players either?

At the last minute it seemed to dawn on us that there was another important occasion just round the corner. But it had also dawned on us how completely exhausted we were. With all the emotional excitement, on top of the energy-sapping conditions, we had run ourselves into the ground and were now paying the penalty. We travelled down to Glasgow on the Friday and stayed at the airport Excelsior Hotel, just as we do for many other games in the Glasgow area. Rangers had won nothing in the 1982–3 season and, with much talk about the future of manager John Greig, this was their last chance to redeem themselves in the eyes of their very demanding supporters.

Winning something, if not everything, every year had become like a divine right to the Ibrox following and they are not too good at accepting that someone else might deserve a turn. Whenever another club gets on top, Rangers are liable to do something dramatic, like sacking a manager. When Celtic had just won the European Cup in 1967, Rangers sacked one of their greatest managers, Scot Symon – on a day when they were actually sitting at the top of the Scottish League!

But if this was their chance to send their fans home happy, they didn't show much sign of scoring the goals which would make that possible. In the whole of that game I can recall only one shot, from Jim Bett, near the end which caused us any problem. Of course it was a thoroughly bad game of football, in which we at least had the reasonable excuse that Gothenburg had taken a lot out of us. We started that final by passing the ball about quite well but the whole occasion just degenerated into one long bore. Even my father, who can raise enthusiasm for almost any game where I'm concerned, couldn't raise a flicker of excitement, so that was my final proof that it was a dreadful game. Nobody was enjoying it and, with no scoring and time running out, we were beginning to dread the thought of a replay. Some of us were due to join the Scottish party for the home internationals and the idea of playing Rangers again on the following Thursday, with Scotland's Canadian tour to follow the home game and running close to Aberdeen's tour of Germany, was all too much for us. There would be no break at all before we were back into the new season. And footballers do need a rest.

We were near the end of extra time when Eric Black saved the day and headed a simple winner for Aberdeen. It was the kind of last-minute victory which the Ibrox team had so often snatched from others in the past. Now that they were no longer a team to be feared, it had happened to them and their fans went streaming home, complaining that the 'Gers had played well enough to win. Well, maybe they had but, as I say, they didn't really trouble us at all.

So we lifted the Scottish Cup with an unusual lack of excitement and headed for St Andrews, which was supposed to be the scene of our celebration that night. Celebration? It was more like a wake! And I didn't help matters by causing an embarrassing scene which I'll come to shortly. On the Sunday we returned to Aberdeen and drove in the now-familiar open-topped bus down Union Street to Pittodrie. Naturally, there was not the large crowd of the Gothenburg day but there was still a surprisingly big turnout, considering the sense of anti-climax after the events of the previous week. Some of us were in a hurry that day. We didn't have long at Pittodrie before we were dashing home for a cup of tea and off to catch the 5.30 p.m. train to Glasgow again. Cars were waiting at Queen Street Station to take us to the Turnberry Hotel, where we joined up with the rest of the Scottish party for the home internationals. Jim Leighton went down by car from Aberdeen but Willie Miller, Alec McLeish, Neil Simpson and myself were on the train and by the time we reached the Ayrshire hotel Jock Stein was taking one look at us and saying it was time for bed.

The first game, with Northern Ireland at Hampden, was not very memorable, except that we were all happy for Neil Simpson getting his first full cap. There was no scoring and we moved on to Porthcawl for the game with Wales at Ninian Park, Cardiff. That produced the better result of Scotland's first win in Wales for many years. One of our two goals was largely a replica of our first goal in Gothenburg. I took a corner on the right and Alec McLeish came running up to head strongly goalwards. Whereas Eric Black had turned to complete the move in Sweden, it was Andy Gray who touched Alec's header home in Cardiff. Big Alec, always happy to score, thought it was his goal but it was definitely Andy's final touch. Feeling better for the experience, we all moved on to the big game with England which had the unusual atmosphere of taking place on a Wednesday evening instead of the traditional Saturday. We had high hopes of winning that game but were beaten 2–0. After that dismal display at Wembley on 1 June, the Scottish party headed straight for Luton airport to fly back to Glasgow. On the way, we passed bus loads of Scots supporters, many of them heading home for work next morning with not much to buck up their spirits from the Wembley result. They looked a pretty dejected bunch, with their Lions Rampant folded away, but the moment they recognized the team bus they suddenly came alive again and started cheering and waving to us. It made us feel even worse that we had not been able to make it a happier night for them but it proved once again that Scotland has the most loyal support in the world.

We buried our disappointment and boarded the plane for Glasgow, where I stayed overnight at the Excelsior Hotel before catching the train north on the Thursday morning. I met up with Lesley at Dundee, where she had been staying with her parents, and we continued the journey back to Aberdeen.

With all the rush of the most hectic season some of us will ever experience, I had not been at Pittodrie for nearly two weeks and I would be off again on the following Tuesday for Scotland's tour of Canada.

So I drove down to the park on the Friday and who did I see coming in through the door but Billy Stark of St Mirren. If I was a bit baffled I didn't have too much time to think about it before the boss himself appeared in the foyer, looking slightly embarrassed that Billy and I had met up before he had time to explain the situation to me. I suppose what was really clicking in my mind was the fact that Billy was a right-midfield player, the same as myself, and that presumably he hadn't come to Aberdeen for his holidays. I knew that Fergie was a long-standing admirer of Billy as a player – he was a goal-scorer among his other talents – and that he had tried to sign him before. As it turned out, Billy had arrived at Pittodrie for the medical examination and final formalities before it was announced to the Press that he had signed for Aberdeen.

The boss's confusion at the meeting between Billy and myself was made all the worse for him because he had

137

just been about to call me in to tear me in shreds for my behaviour on the night of the Scottish Cup Final. Aberdeen fans don't have to be reminded that, despite the fact that we had just won the cup, the boss had launched into a tirade at the Press conference about a disgraceful performance, stating that only Willie Miller and Alec McLeish had played at all. What he said to the Press was nothing compared to what he had already said to the players in the dressing room. For a start, when he came in, he stopped me from opening a bottle of champagne so that he could begin to tear a strip off us all, except Willie and Alec. Actually, Alec McLeish arrived late in the dressing room and, totally unaware of the boss's fury, launched into a celebration shout of 'Great stuff, lads!' Suddenly, in the gloom of the dressing room, he realized he had said something wrong. So the heads were down and the mood was more like a funeral than a celebration of the fact that we had just won the country's national cup a few minutes earlier. In doing so, we had made history as the only team except Rangers and Celtic to win it two years in succession.

All right, I can understand the boss's frustration that we hadn't played well, but whatever criticism could be levelled at us, nobody could say we weren't giving all we had. But frankly, at the end of that fantastic season, there wasn't a lot left to give. We had battled away for the league title and nearly won it. We had run through the whole excitement and superhuman effort of the European Cup Winners' Cup – and won it, remember? We had played our hearts out for Aberdeen and many of the lads had come to the end of their tether for one season.

There is only so much the human body can take. In fairness to the boss, he quickly realized he had been less than fair to his players and apologized next day. But by then the damage had been done. There was no real sense of celebration on that night of winning the Scottish Cup for the fourth time in the club's history and even less anticipation of going down Union Street to what would be a bit of an anticlimax after the hundred thousand welcomes which had greeted us back from Gothenburg. From Hampden we had headed for the Old Course Hotel at St Andrews where we were joined by our wives for what was meant to be the celebration function. The bus journey was a most depressing business. Players like John McMaster were really down and Stuart Kennedy, who had had a tragic enough end to his season anyway by missing out on Gothenburg, was even worse. The silence on the bus was broken occasionally by somebody trying to make a joke about Willie and Alec having won the game on their own. One joker said they would only need a tandem to cycle down Union Street to salute the public! Mr Donald, the chairman, came along and tried to cheer us up but the mood was already set.

When it came to the St Andrews reception, the atmosphere was so bad that I said to Lesley, 'Come on, we're going.' We got up and walked out of the function and our departure was certainly noticed. Much as I like and respect Alec Ferguson – and I mean that very sincerely – I felt he had treated his players in a way they did not deserve and this was my way of getting back at him, my personal show of protest. Of course, almost immediately I realized I had been headstrong and shouldn't have done it. I later apologized to the rest of the boys.

Most of all, I was upset by the embarrassment I must have caused Mr Donald and Mr Anderson, the chairman and vice-chairman, because they certainly didn't deserve anything like that, having treated us all so well and run the club so efficiently all those years. But I suppose there are times when something gets to you like that and you act on impulse. I knew the players at Pittodrie were not the kind to cause a manager problems by going out drinking or anything like that. You cannot guarantee that your quality of football will be a hundred per cent – nobody can do that – but you can guarantee maximum effort and I knew that on that score nobody could fault the lads at Pittodrie.

It was inevitable that I would be called to answer for

my behaviour at St Andrews but with all the international commitments, I had not seen the boss to speak to. Now the moment had arrived and here was Billy Stark slightly complicating the matter for him.

'Just wait there a minute, Billy,' he called as he summoned me into his office and proceeded to tell me that, because of my display of bad manners, I would be fined £250. Fines are not uncommon, though the public never hear of them at Pittodrie, but I told him I realized I had made a fool of myself and that fining me £250 wasn't going to make things any different. However the fine stood and we moved on to the next thing on his mind – the explanation of Billy Stark's appearance.

'I'm about to sign Billy,' said Fergie.

'Oh yes,' I replied. 'He's a very good player but it just makes it all the more crowded around the midfield.'

'But you are anxious to leave Aberdeen, aren't you?' he said.

'Well I'm thinking about leaving when my contract is up but that's a year away yet and I will do the club the courtesy of waiting to hear what they have to offer me first.'

If I had had any doubts on the matter, I was then thoroughly convinced that the signing of Billy Stark was a preparation for my departure. I had certainly made it clear that I thought I should further my career beyond Pittodrie, much as I loved the Northeast and enjoyed playing for the Dons. If I were as good a player as many people were saying, then it was natural that I would want to secure the kind of financial future that can be provided by only a very few clubs in England and some others on the Continent. Make no mistake about it, Aberdeen reward their top players better than any other club in Scotland and there must be only four or five clubs in England who can top it. Money apart, I needed the challenge of playing outside the Scottish Premier League and testing myself against a broader spectrum of teams. Altogether, it was shaping up to the fact that I would very likely be leaving Pittodrie in 1984 and, since Alec

Ferguson is one of the shrewdest men in the game, the same thought had obviously occurred to him. By signing Billy Stark he was not only strengthening his pool, as he publicly stated, but was insuring against my departure by bringing in a player who would perform much the same kind of function. I wondered at the time if he might not be thinking it would be economically better to put the word around that I was available since he could demand a better price for the club if I were still under contract. For my part, I was perfectly happy to play out my contract, completing nearly seven seasons at Pittodrie and taking my chance after that.

23

Jock Stein's Anger

Billy Stark was duly signed and the public read all about it next day. I went home and packed my bags for the Canadian tour. Against the fact that it had been such a long and hard season I was fired with enthusiasm because I was adding to my number of international caps and I had never been to North America. I was also delighted by the news that Jock Stein had called Mark McGhee into the Scottish pool for the first time. At twenty-six, Mark deserved a chance to play for his country. He had already been told he would be on stand-by in case of withdrawals and even put back the date of his wedding to make sure it wouldn't interfere with his chances of playing for Scotland. When John Wark and Alan Brazil said they would not be going to Canada I knew that Mark would now get his chance and we were all very happy for him. He and I, Willie Miller and Alec McLeish all met up and flew from Dyce to Heathrow, where we met up with Jim Leighton and the rest of the Scottish party.

It was in London that someone mentioned boots and I went into a cold sweat. 'Boots?'

'Yes boots, those things you wear on your feet to play football.'

I swallowed hard and realized that, in all my careful packing, I had come away without a single item of footwear – rubber boots, screw-in boots, training shoes or anything. I was scared to tell Jock Stein so I decided to keep it quiet and contact the Adidas man as soon as we got to Vancouver. Mr Stein found out, however, and took it not too badly, passing it off with some sarcastic remark like 'Good professional, son!'

With a stop at Calgary, we completed the long journey to Vancouver, made all the more fascinating because we had followed the sun all the way from London and arrived with the same daylight as we had left. Scotland had come for a three-match tour of Canada, a country needing a boost to its football interest and now preparing to test its national team against us in Vancouver, B.C., Edmonton, Alberta, and Toronto, Ontario. We settled at the West-Inn on Vancouver's Bay Shore, a beautiful setting with a magnificent view of the rich people's yachts and the strange contrast of the warm weather and the sight of the snowcapped Rocky Mountains. When you make a journey like that it is often difficult to sleep and this was no exception. Mark and I shared a room and we lay and watched Canadian television for the first time. Willie and Alec share a room on these occasions and Jim Leighton was with his rival for the goalkeeping position, Billy Thomson of St Mirren. The hotel, incidentally, had a plaque to say that Howard Hughes had slept there!

The Aberdeen boys didn't go out much though most of us went to the horse-racing, a sport I had never sampled before. We trained on that much-publicized astroturf which gave some of the players blisters on their feet. It was worn and felt like a mixture of concrete and ice, very disconcerting and not at all to our liking. It was evidently the worst artificial surface in North America and was soon to be replaced by something much better in the magnificent new stadium which had just been built but was not yet open.

We saw the new place and it was easily the most magnificent stadium I had ever seen. We thought the Olympic Stadium in Munich was some place but it had nothing on the Vancouver one. We had to settle for that dreadful artificial turf in the old ground and I got some stuff to put on my feet. Because it was his first chance to play for Scotland, Mark McGhee was naturally trying to make an impression but the more he did so the more damage he was doing his feet. They were in such a bad state I didn't think he would be able to play on. But it is amazing the lengths to which you will go to earn your first cap. All credit to him. After Charlie Nicholas had been pulled down for the penalty, from which I scored our opening goal, Mark came on to replace Charlie and scored a very fine second one. But it was a scrappy game. Before we left Vancouver I played golf in a valley of the Rockies. It was there that a chap told me a story which gave me second thoughts about searching for any ball in the rough. Last time he did that, he found himself face to face with a bear. Mind you, I don't know if that would have been any more alarming than the dressing-down which Jock Stein gave us all before that first match in Canada.

Usually when something like that is about to happen the rumour gets around but on that occasion it came right out of the blue. With the memory of the home internationals behind us, he called us in to say he was not satisfied he was getting enough from the players. He started by saying there was no pressure on him; he could look after himself but he was dissatisfied with us. He was not exactly screaming but I had never heard him angry like that. Personally, I didn't agree with what he was saying about lack of effort because I know that, as far as the Aberdeen boys at least are concerned, there is never any lack of that. We tackle hard even in training, a practice some of the Anglos don't like. On top of Mr Stein's tirade, his assistant, the inimitable Jim McLean, came on the scene and he was even more forceful.

'If anybody wants to say anything, say it now!' was his opening blast.

I piped up and said I thought the training schedule with Scotland could be harder than it was. Certainly we trained a lot harder at Pittodrie. But Jock Stein likes you to rest. I like the Aberdeen routine for a Wednesday match, for example, where you get up in the morning, do a bit of training and breathing of the fresh air and go back to bed in the afternoon. I find that, if you don't get up till midday on a match day there is a lethargy which follows you around. Anyway, according to the Press reports, we came out of that showdown meeting with the manager looking ashen-faced. Willie Miller was interviewed and said we had all accepted the criticism.

As I said, this was my first time in North America and I was getting used to the size and scope of everything, including their big, daft cars. I was also getting used to the fact that Scots are more Scottish abroad, coming up to us and saying things like 'Aye, Jimmy' and 'You're right there, pal!' As you might expect, we had to go through the ceremony of being piped off the plane at Vancouver even though we had just had a long, tiring flight.

At least Vancouver was an attractive city, which was more than could be said for Edmonton, Alberta, which didn't seem to have much to commend it except the Commonwealth stadium and the fact that we would be playing on grass instead of that threadbare, artificial stuff. The Canadian team followed us on to Edmonton and when we met them for our second encounter, the referee distinguished himself by cutting the first half short by nearly five minutes. He then made things worse by coming into our dressing room and offering to play the lost minutes at the start of the second half before turning us round to play the remaining forty-five minutes in the other direction! You should have heard the way Mr Stein told him not to be daft, or words to that effect. An accompanying linesman shrugged in embarrassment and said it wasn't his idea. I hadn't particularly wanted to play in that game because of very sore eyes but the boss said some people would be wanting to see me and he would play me for part of the game anyway. In that second half the referee began to lose the place even more than in the shortened first half. Both sides were complaining about his bad decisions and I eventually gave him some verbals about his timekeeping, which was meant to be a joke. So he booked me, as well as Charlie Nicholas and Roy Aitken, and I was taken off. The boss was displeased that I had blotted my copybook after having kept a clean sheet for eighteen months. Right enough, it was stupid because it could have gone against me in the future. We beat the Canadians 3–0, with goals from Charlie Nicholas, Richard Gough and Graeme Souness but I was glad to see the back of Edmonton, not least for the fact that Mark McGhee and I spent so much time in our room, ordering cups of tea at £2 a time and making long phone calls home, that we ran up a record room-service bill of 260 dollars.

Toronto revived our spirits. We were staying at the fashionable Hilton Hotel on the lakeside, the weather was good and this was where you really found the Scottish exiles out in force. There were Scottish banners everywhere as the boys took the field. You could nearly have mistaken it for Hampden. Rangers and Celtic supporters' clubs were there in large numbers and there was even a Partick Thistle supporter in evidence. With an eye infection, I was kept on the bench for the first half while Andy Gray was suddenly hitting form and scoring two goals. By the time I was put on in the second half the game had died and it seemed to me that players were simply going through the motions. Personally, I was trying shots at goal from forty yards, which didn't please Mr Stein at all. Along with Roy Aitken and Tommy Burns I went along to a supporters' buffet reception where we were given a great welcome, accompanied by bagpipes as ever. Tommy, Roy, Mark and I went about a lot together and on our last day we landed in one of those photo studios where you can dress up and have your picture taken in the old Wild West styles. Tommy Burns had always dreamed about being Davy Crockett (even though he doesn't shoot so well!) so he donned the big furry cap and we ended up in one of those serious poker-faced poses in sepia colouring.

From the home internationals onwards Charlie Nicholas was involved in all those talks about his future.

Would the new wonder-boy of Scottish football be leaving Celtic? Where was he going? Managers and agents were buzzing around the team camps and there was a lot of talk about the effect of all this on the rest of the Scottish players.

Actually Charlie kept his problems very well to himself for a lad of his age and we weren't really upset by all that was happening. We did begin to get the drift of where he might be going – Liverpool, Manchester United or Arsenal. Old Trafford had always been his own personal ambition but we gathered he was not too impressed with manager Ron Atkinson and it was therefore no surprise when he ended up at Highbury.

Another Press talking-point seemed to be the form of Billy Thomson, the St Mirren goalkeeper, who had been preferred to our own Jim Leighton for the opening game in Vancouver. Apparently he was adapting better to the artificial surface. The boss was no doubt trying to keep Jim on his toes and there was quite a lot of speculation by the Glasgow journalists in particular about a serious threat to Jim's position. Frankly, that kind of speculation didn't impress me at all. To me, Jim Leighton has been the best goalkeeper in Scotland for years and I couldn't see that Billy, good keeper though he is, had done anything to endanger his position.

Naturally, after such a long and hard season for many of us, there was a lot of discussion about the value and wisdom of a tour like the Canadian one. I found it valuable for what it produced in team spirit, which was easily the best I have ever known in a Scottish squad. On a tour like that you get to know the people who can travel and mix well and, believe me, these things are important.

The public see us only on the field and naturally imagine that playing skill is all there is to it. But footballers are human beings, with all the usual passions and weaknesses, and it matters that they like each other and get on together. In all honesty, we were not tested as footballers and ended up in the last game with centre backs playing in midfield.

147

Much as I appreciated playing for Scotland again and seeing North America for the first time, it was good to get back home. A season of incredible success and excitement had really gone on too long and I was badly in need of the first holiday I had had since coming to Aberdeen five years earlier. We would soon be back in training but before then Lesley and I would be attending the Queen's Garden Party at Holyroodhouse in my native Edinburgh and I would be heading back across the Atlantic with my four-year-old son Gavin.

As I tried to make the most of the short break from football, two pieces of news which we had learned while in Canada began to sink in. First, Aberdeen had been voted the Best Team in Europe in the annual awards decided by the sports manufacturers Adidas and the magazine *France Football*. With our various successes, we had pipped the European Cup Winners, Hamburg, for the supreme honour and that was some achievement. Secondly, we had heard that our Pittodrie boss, Alec Ferguson, was likely to sign a lucrative five-year contract to stay with Aberdeen, ending speculation that he might be going to a big English club or even to his old club, Rangers. The Aberdeen lads were delighted with the news.

Whatever players may sometimes say about their manager, Fergie had proved himself by his deeds. In less than five years at Pittodrie he had taken us to the Premier League Championship, a European Cup Winners' Cup triumph, two successive Scottish Cup wins and two more League Cup finals, achieving more in that short period than all the previous nine managers had achieved in seventy-five years. Who could doubt the man's record? Even before coming north he had succeeded in building what most people would say was the best St Mirren team in the Love Street history, signing players like McGarvey, Fitzpatrick and Weir and keeping them for years as part of a team which gained regular success against Celtic, Rangers and Aberdeen.

I must confess I had really expected that Fergie would

leave Aberdeen and the talk of his five-year contract surprised me. So he seemed there to stay. With my own contract expiring at the end of the 1983–4 season, would I still be at Pittodrie a year from now? I would be facing the new season with a distinct hunch that I was starting out on my last year at Aberdeen. With Billy Stark now signed, would the club try to sell me before my contract was up, avoiding any reference to a tribunal? All that was in the future but at least the Dons could be sure of maximum performance as usual in the coming season. As I have said, I would not be rushing away without hearing their offer but, if it turned out that I was in the shop window, then I would have to prove to potential buyers that I was worth buying. Whatever happened, there would be interesting times ahead.

24

Top Hat and Tails

Lesley and I had been invited to the Royal Garden Party in Edinburgh and you should have seen me all decked out in my top hat and tails as we headed down the Royal Mile to the Queen's big 'do'. Inside the grounds of Holyrood I was holding my top hat in my hand when I noticed people looking inside it. I then realized there was a large No. 12 on the silk, a code number for the hire company and for me, as one high-class wag commented, a place on the substitutes' bench. Not being accustomed to posh affairs like a Royal Garden Party, I stood up on a chair to get a better look at the Queen. When you are my size you don't stand much of a chance of a view over a sea of lum-hats. I was aware of a few toffs frowning at my conduct but it wasn't long before they were all tumbling to the idea and getting up on chairs themselves.

Once that was over, Gavin and I set out for Florida, on a promise to visit Disney World with his dad who had been away from home so much in recent months. With her dislike of flying, Lesley was staying at home with little Craig. At London, we were standing in a queue when a chap from Air Florida came up and asked if I would care to pose for a photograph with some of the stewardesses (Gothenburg fame was following us around). So I obliged and the next I knew we were being conveyed to the v.i.p. lounge and ushered to the first-class cabin of the plane. Surprises had begun even before we reached Disneyland. We flew to Miami and Orlando and settled in for a great ten days at the Holiday Inn. We were like a couple of kids, not just one. We explored the famous Sea World as well as the wonders of Disney for hours on end till I was half asleep, saying to Gavin at eight o'clock at night, 'Where are we now, son?' Among the joys of Orlando was the Wet and Wild amusement arcade with its bobsleigh runs and so on. It seemed the last place in the world I would ever meet anyone I knew. Well, I didn't exactly meet him but I discovered to my horror that Fergie had been there the previous day. I'll tell you, since he had fined me for my behaviour at the Cup Final reception at St Andrews, I was keeping well out of his way. However, I couldn't keep out of the way of a big black Cadillac which screeched to a halt as Gavin and I were leaving the arcade one day. The driver rolled down his window – and who did it turn out to be but Martin Buchan. The former Aberdeen and Manchester United captain was there on holiday with his wife and family. His stoppage was holding up the traffic but we managed to exchange a few greetings and to leave our longer chat till Aberdeen played United in Martin's testimonial at Old Trafford in the pre-season match some weeks later. It sure is a small world.

When Gavin and I flew back from Florida there was just enough time to take Lesley to London for a long weekend before we would be off on that pre-season Dons' trip to Switzerland and Germany.

In London we stayed with Stevie and Maureen Archibald, with whom we had been friendly in their Aberdeen days. They had just had their second baby and were between selling one house and buying another. So they were living temporarily in the home of Rikki Villa, the famous Argentinian who had recently left Spurs to play for Fort Lauderdale in America. The four of us went out for a meal at one of those showbusiness restaurants where the chap at the next table was the comedian Kelly Monteith.

Naturally, Stevie was asking what I intended to do when my contract was up and I said that, much as I liked Aberdeen and would keep a base there, I would

likely want to move on. People have said that contact
with people like Steve Archibald tends to unsettle players
in Scotland who are earning much less. But, as I have
already said, that honestly has never troubled me. Of
course you want to build up as much security as possible
for your family, knowing that football is such a short life,
but I have never allowed my head to be turned by any
big talk from the south. For example, I didn't envy Stevie
the fact that he was obviously very much at home in the
posh restaurants of London. I was paying the bill and
when I asked him what I should leave for a tip, he
suggested ten pounds. Maybe I have become a cautious
Aberdonian but I decided that a fiver was enough! Even
that was my tipping budget for the whole weekend used
up in one go. At that time Stevie seemed quite happy
with Spurs, though there had been mention of friction
between himself and the manager, but within a few
weeks of our visit he was asking for a transfer and
obviously feeling quite unsettled. As I say, you can never
plan too far ahead in football. Despite his higher income
and more high-flying life in London, I'm sure Stevie
would have given his eyeteeth to have been part of our
great night in Gothenburg.

25

Martin's Big Night

Immediately after our London break, I was off on the Dons' continental tour which turned out to be far too long. The boss himself was the first to admit it was a mistake. For those of us who had been through that long hard season at home, with the pressures of Europe, the home internationals and the Canadian tour, it had become all too much. With a ridiculously short break, here we were on another seventeen-day trip to the Continent. Even the lads who had not been involved in the international matches felt the strain of being away from home all that time. We were neither sharp enough nor in the right frame of mind. The fact that we recorded some poor results did our image no good, even though the teams we were playing were far better than their names suggested. German standards are so high that you find lesser teams which could compete quite well in our Premier League. Everybody was being given the chance of a game so there was no settled pattern about the team. In one spell we played four games in five days and in the final of the main competition we simply couldn't raise our game and were beaten by Dinamo Bucharest 2–0.

We were due to play a special fixture in the city of Nuremberg, where Hitler used to hold his rallies. That became quite an experience for me. The German newspapers had been giving me some attention since we knocked Bayern out of the Cup Winners' Cup and now they were linking my name with the team we were about to play. One very influential German journalist was writing an open letter to the Nuremberg president advising him to sell his jet plane and buy me! Poor chap. I tried to pay as little attention to the publicity as possible. We arrived at the Nuremberg ground, changed into our strip and headed for the tunnel. I was last man out and just as I was about to run on to the pitch, a little man in a pinstriped suit stopped me and said, 'You like Nuremberg?'

I said, 'Yes, very nice.'

'You like the city? You like the park?'

'Yes, yes.'

I was being as polite as I could to the stranger. Just as I broke away from him, his last piece of information was 'I am the president, you see.'

I ran as fast as possible before the boss could see me in conversation with the Nuremberg president. Evidently the local supporters were believing the publicity and were cheering me every time I touched the ball, as if I were soon to become one of their players. They are not one of the big names in Europe but their status corresponds to Hearts in that they were once a powerful side in the land and have fallen on harder times. But they are on a bigger scale. Even now, Nuremberg draw crowds of 25,000 and have the potential of matching Manchester United's 50,000. Although I would have been thinking more of Hamburg or Bayern Munich in any move to the Continent, I would also have had to give serious thought to Nuremberg. Whether they actually made official inquiries or not I never discovered because, as I have said, Alec Ferguson doesn't often tell us; I think his policy is right. Unless a manager has real intentions of selling a player there is no point in diverting his attention from the job on hand. If you ask, he says he gets inquiries about every player in the team. Back home, however, the rumours persisted. We were playing Arsenal, Ipswich and Manchester United in our final run-up to the new season and, on the day of the match at Old Trafford, the *Daily Star* said I was going to Arsenal. It was the first I had heard of it and, of course, it came to nothing.

The visit to Old Trafford was rather a special occasion. Martin Buchan had been a great servant of both Aberdeen and United and became the only player in history to captain a winning team in both the Scottish and English Cup Finals. This was his farewell testimonial and what a happy coincidence that the two clubs he had captained should oblige by winning those two cups again in the same year. It was the perfect set-up for a play-off between the cup winners of Scotland and England, a match in which national pride would make sure it was more than just a friendly kick-around. I had never been to Old Trafford before and was impressed by the layout. In the first half, United gained supremacy and were two goals up at the interval. With defeats from Arsenal and Ipswich behind us, on top of the mediocre performances in Germany, we badly needed to redeem ourselves before the English dismissed our Gothenburg victory as something of a fluke. The boss was obviously aware of all that at half-time and our second-half performance was something different.

Whatever United did to us in the first half, we more than did to them in the second. Peter Weir scored twice to draw us level and came so close to scoring a winner. For my own part, I managed to turn on some of my best little tricks and had the United defence running in circles. Martin Buchan's family were down from Aberdeen and attended a reception afterwards when Martin presented us all with quartz watches. It was a very happy Northeast night in Manchester. On the football field, our honour had been saved and the result became more significant on the following Saturday when United played Liverpool in the Charity Shield at Wembley (Cup holders versus League Champions) and beat them 2–0.

That was the opening day of the season in Scotland and we played Dundee at Pittodrie with our confidence restored, beating them 3–0. The fact that I was badly injured that day and was out of the team for weeks was a huge disappointment because I knew I was right back on form. The boss reckoned I was playing my best football. When I went down with that injury, incidentally, the Dundee players were howling at the referee to book me for taking a dive. A dive? They had been giving me a bit of treatment all afternoon and I reckon I saved some of them a booking because I got up in some pain and shook their hands. Finally young McKinlay crocked me, tearing ligaments from toes to ankle and putting me out of the game for too long. The lad was no doubt tired towards the end of the game but that doesn't make it any less galling when people suggest you are play-acting. I was injured all right.

It was only the second time in my career I had been put out of the game by a direct kicking. My injuries are more often strains. No matter how good a player you may be or what ambitions you may have beyond the club you play for, the important thing is to be an active and valuable member of the team as often as possible. Many a talented footballer who has been injured or has lost form has found himself out in the cold and forgotten about. It can happen very easily. When I had my long lay-off the Dons had a phenomenal run of success without me and that helps to keep your feet on the ground and make you realize that you are not indispensable. I would always hope that I can add something extra to an Aberdeen performance but there is so much talent at Pittodrie that you can never take anything for granted.

So it was at the start of the 1983–4 season when I found myself out of the game. Although I had played in that 3–0 win over Dundee, the team proceeded to score another twenty-one goals without losing a single one and I had no part in it. When you are out of the swim you become more edgy and, in my own case, it meant that I was thinking more and more about the future. I must admit my thoughts were now geared to the idea that I would be leaving Aberdeen, although I had had wonderful years there, had made so many good friends and would probably never find such a nice place to stay. As a

Above: Familiar faces at a charity night in Jimmy Wilson's bar immediately after the Bayern victory. As well as Sir Hugh Fraser (right) and myself, there was Chalky Whyte, Jimmy Wilson, Joe Harper (ex-Dons), Chris Kay (Grampian TV), Willie Hunter (ex-Motherwell), Ian St John (ex-Motherwell and Liverpool) and Tommy McMillan (ex-Don). At the front: Ian Taylor (ex-Don) and John Fitzpatrick (ex-Manchester United)

Below left: Alex Ferguson, the Boss

Below right: Those incredible crowd scenes in Union Street as we returned from Gothenburg with the European Cup Winners' Cup in May 1983

Back where it all started — Peter Weir and I display the European Cup Winners' Cup to the crowds at Pittodrie

sign that I was not planning to break the connection altogether, I bought a second home in the city in the autumn of 1983 and moved in there, leaving my bigger house in Albury Road for letting. Whatever happened, I felt I would keep on both houses.

At the very least they would be an investment. At the most I would have somewhere to return to when my football days were over. Friends and advisers like Bob Law and Bill Scullion, insurance experts, had kept me right on matters like that. I was training as hard as ever – the boss would vouch for that – but I was finding it harder to concentrate on the Premier League.

By the time I was approaching my twenty-seventh birthday, I had to admit that money was beginning to look more important than it did when I was twenty-five. You are thinking more and more about security. What about the wife and kids? Football is a very different occupation from most others. The man on the terracing will probably hold his job until retirement. Even if he does something dramatically wrong he will likely have the protection of his trade union. A footballer's livelihood is dependent on his performances week by week. No room here for a drop in productivity. Nor is there a guarantee of a place in next Saturday's eleven. If someone else fills the place better or even if the manager just happens to prefer his face, no amount of pleading to the Players' Union for unfair dismissal can possibly do anything for you. What you learn quite early in football is that you are on your own. Clubs like Aberdeen will go on for ever but the players who pass through their ranks can be forgotten in a short time. Some may buy a pub and become their own best customers. Others may be misled in a business deal and find themselves in the bankruptcy court before they know what has happened. When I have had a lingering injury I have lain in bed at night, tossing and turning and wondering what I would do if it all came to a sudden end.

Just when I'm thinking I know of no other way that I could make a living, I give myself a pinch and say 'Well, if big Doug Baillie can be a sportswriter, so could you!'

As I say, though you combine with your team-mates on a Saturday afternoon, it is really every man for himself after that. Whatever the future may hold for me in the playing sense, I sometimes look beyond that and think I may end up with a sports shop. I had some invaluable experience when Donald McIntosh engaged me to work part-time at Rosslyn Sports. I got to know something about the trade and to know the company representatives who used to call. I was never any good at pub talk so that wouldn't be my line. And I don't fancy becoming the employee of a brewery company. Willie Miller did it the right way when he and a relative bought over Jimmy Wilson's hostelry and made it their own enterprise.

26

Gothenburg Lolly

In expressing fears about future security, I would be the last to deny that football has been good to me and that many of us are better off than the average citizen will ever be. At the same time, any idea that Aberdeen players became very rich men as a result of the European Cup Winners' Cup triumph is very far off the mark. A lot of rumours circulated after Gothenburg but you would be surprised at what was left after tax. Let's just say we had one very good year which might never come to any of us again.

The facts are that, for anyone who played in all those European games and collected all the bonuses, the gross earnings in the Gothenburg year came to between £30,000 and £35,000. That certainly sounds like a lot of money but there are players in England earning £50,000 or even £100,000 for winning nothing. In my own case, as I mentioned earlier, I was pursued by Charlie Nicholas's agent, Bev Walker, after my success in the World Cup and that could no doubt have earned me a lot more. But I decided to stick to something more modest and channel any extra earnings into a company called Gordon Strachan Enterprises. I have written regular columns for the *Scottish Daily Express* and *Match Weekly* but beyond that I have not spent too much time on my outside activities. I'm on contract to wear Adidas boots and I have had the free run of a car from a firm in Stonehaven.

Other commercial interests have tended to bring as

much laughter as lolly but they have all been good experience which I shall keep in mind for any future enterprises of my own. They used to advertise that 'Gordon Strachan runs on oil – supplied by Ellis and McHardy', which meant that I was offered oil for my central heating. As it happened I didn't need the oil so I did a swop for coal instead. The result was that I accumulated a couple of lorry-loads of coal, which I promptly gave away to my mother-in-law.

Then there was the company which supplies fitted kitchens and approached me before Gothenburg about using my name to promote their equipment. We were not all that keen to be fitted with a new kitchen – our own one was perfectly good – but we agreed and awaited the arrival of the man. Lesley began clearing out the contents of her cupboards but there was never any sign of the kitchen man. We phoned several times to see if he was really coming until it all became a bit of a joke. But it became even funnier on the last call when a secretary explained that they had heard I might be leaving Scotland to play in the German league. Now her director wanted to know if I could give them a guarantee that I would be with Aberdeen for at least another year. Otherwise they had lost their enthusiasm for giving me a kitchen. I tried not to be rude to the girl but how could I give a guarantee like that? The boss might decide to transfer me any day. Could you imagine a big transfer deal being negotiated and me butting in to say: 'I'm sorry, I really can't go just now. You see, I've promised a kitchen company. . . .' The thing was a farce and Lesley quietly put the things back in her cupboards and got nothing but a sore back for her troubles.

Other players' commercial activities produce their laughs too. I mean, what do you make of big Doug Rougvie and his cream cakes? He got a lot of leg-pulling about those advertisements in the newspapers and on the radio when he confessed, 'Yes, it is true I have a weakness – it's for cream cakes.' On the opening day of the 1983–4 season I called to the big man, 'Hey, Doug,

Peter Mackie of Dundee has found a new way to get past you today. There he is, running out and carrying a tray of cream cakes!' The big bear just grinned his toothless grin.

Willie Miller has done quite well with sponsorship and Stuart Kennedy and Alec McLeish have had cars. But I sometimes cringe with embarrassment when I think of the players who don't get their share of these perks. It would be nice to think there was someone who recognized that a genius like John McMaster has already given twelve years of devoted service to Aberdeen.

In connection with our European success, of course, there was a team commercial effort, run by Proscot from Glasgow. That produced one major laugh when we made the 'European Song' recording at North Sound studios in King's Gate. I thought I knew my team-mates pretty well, but their attempts at singing gave me a whole new slant on their personalities. That takes me back to big Doug, the cream-cake man, who had been a close friend of Andy Watson for years. They were standing together, all set for the recording session, when the big man let out his first musical screech. I thought Andy was going to burst himself laughing. The tears were rolling down his cheeks. Derek Hamilton had a good voice and Alec McLeish was none too bad but most of the rest of us were a cause for laughter. Stuart Kennedy opened his mouth and let out a noise which was a cross between a Lee Marvin impersonation and a belly-rumble. It might have been a relief to him but it was painful to us. By some miracle of recording camouflage they managed to make it sound a great record, tuneful and bouncy and I believe they sold upwards of 30,000 copies. My elder boy, Gavin, went to his nursery school on the day after it was released with dreams of a pop-star pop and apparently asked the class, 'Has anyone heard my Dad's latest record?'

27

The Boys in Red

Most people tell us that the pool of players built up by Alec Ferguson has been the best ever seen at Pittodrie and I suppose our victory in Europe bears that out. It has certainly been a great privilege to play with such a talented bunch of lads, displaying such a wide range of talents.

Whatever else happens at Pittodrie, the Gothenburg team has written its way into history. Their names will be remembered and talked about long after they have parted company with football. So maybe I can give my assessment of them now, not only as players but as people, on and off the park.

Alec Ferguson will go down as one of the greatest managers British football has ever seen. With very limited resources he built up St Mirren's finest team. Then he went on to repeat the performance at Aberdeen, paying big money for only one of his players, Peter Weir, whom he had raised as a lad at St Mirren. Even without that track record, I would still put him down as the best football tactician I have ever come across. What's more, despite the fact that we have had our differences of opinion and he has had to discipline me, I really like the man. His patter is brilliant. Oh, he's a hard, hard man – they don't come any harder – but when it's relaxation time he joins in with the lads and can take a joke against himself as well as give it out.

You can never be quite sure of his mood, except after a

bad result when there are no prizes for guessing what it will be. There are days when he will walk right past you as if you didn't exist. I usually know the days when he is all right. He comes in and starts calling me Ugly Face. That's his favourite name for me. I can then relax and pass word round among the boys, 'The boss is in a good mood today.' The one thing you must never do with Fergie is tell him lies. He expects you to be straightforward and you will suffer if you are not.

Archie Knox, Fergie's assistant who has since become manager of Dundee, was the loud man of Pittodrie, the shouter. If we arrived in the morning and the place was all quiet, we said, 'Is Archie away somewhere today?' There was never any doubt about his presence. But he has a great sense of humour and he's an absolute workhorse who lives for his football. There is a rumour that he occasionally sends his wife a photograph of himself to remind her what he looks like. It could be true for he lives, eats and shouts football. If there was a game of rats versus mice in the carpark he would be across there giving them the benefit of his wisdom. He obviously picked up a lot of the basics from Jim McLean, when he was with Dundee United, and turned them into managerial success when he went to Forfar. He even swears like Jim McLean. But like McLean and Fergie, he knows the game inside out, to the extent that he was always capable of taking on a top team of his own, as has now happened. I was playing in a reserve match recently and had the doubtful privilege of being taken there in the club's mini-bus, with Archie as the driver. He tends to go round corners with the same determination that he shows in his football.

With the small crowd at a reserve game, you heard him all the louder. At this particular one I could hear him bellowing in exasperation from the dugout, 'You're getting on my tits, Tam!' That was one of his politer remarks. Afterwards he drove us home at high speed once more. Somebody wanted music and asked if he

163

would put on the tapes.

'Tapes?' he roared. 'That's all you lot have in your heads. The way some of you were playing there tonight it looked as if you were listening to music instead of playing football.'

Jim Leighton has no real competition as a goalkeeper in Scotland. In fact only Peter Shilton is a better keeper in Britain today and Jim could be set to take over that position. His natural ability is fantastic and he has worked hard at reaching his international place. I sit beside Jim in the dressing room on training days and we have a lot of good-humoured banter. When he arrives at Pittodrie in the morning his hair is sticking in all directions. I pull his leg and ask if he had a hard time in the coffin last night. Glenn Hoddle told Steve Archibald he thought Aberdeen were the ugliest team he had ever seen and I said to Steve, 'He must have been looking at Jim Leighton and Doug Rougvie.' But Jim won't hear of himself being classed with Doug and claims that it's me who needs some good-look tablets to catch up with the pair of them. Nickname for Jim: Bozo.

Stuart Kennedy I regard as one of the main reasons I have done well at Pittodrie. I have played bad balls and been amazed at the speed with which he could make them look better than they were. Stuart, who is my room-mate when we travel, is a thorough professional, a teetotaller, nonsmoker and fitness fanatic, which explains why, as the oldest man in the Aberdeen squad, he could outpace the best of them on those darting runs up the wing. If he has a fault, it is that he will never accept that he has had a bad game. Mostly he is right, of course, because he very seldom has. He has a very ready wit and shrewd brain which he applies to various activities, including the buying and selling of property. He is also the Secret Service of the club, with a complete knowledge of all that is going on. He'll tell the young boys on Monday morning, 'I know what you were up to at the weekend,'

164

and from there he gathers up one piece of information after another. He, Alec McLeish, John McMaster and myself are the card-playing partners at the back of the team bus. Nickname: Kiddie.

Doug Rougvie is, because of his gigantic proportions and flailing limbs, sometimes regarded as a dirty player, but I can honestly say I have never seen him injure a player deliberately. I would go as far as to say I have never known a more gentle man. He is a delightful big guy who is great with kids and he just dotes on his own daughter who has the same big, open smile as her dad. The Aberdeen crowd love him, I think partly because of a wish to be like him – big and strong and conducting himself with abandon. There's a touch of the Superman about it.

They encourage him with that Zulu-like call of 'Roogvee-Roogvee' and whenever he hears the chant his nostrils flare, his chest goes out and off he goes on one of his famous runs. When that happens, there is no stopping him. He becomes inspired like a giant who doesn't know his own strength. The rest of us just wave him goodbye and hope to see him later. But he's a great chap to have on your side, an enthusiast of great good humour and the kind of character who is badly needed in the game today. He has never kidded himself about being a great footballer but his experience in recent years has given him the confidence to be a much better player than most people ever thought possible. He is a classic example of what can be done with endeavour. In an age when there are too many dour, determined, serious faces in football, big Doug is the smiling face of the game, a man so much in love with his football that he lives for every Saturday and can't wait to get down that tunnel. Nickname: The Bat, for the way he sometimes takes off on those low, full-length dives.

John McMaster is a great player whom the Aberdeen supporters have taken a long time to recognize. Here, if ever, is a man who should have been playing for

GORDON STRACHAN: AN AUTOBIOGRAPHY

Scotland, with that magnificent left foot and the ability to know exactly what he is going to do with the ball before it reaches him. Only that dreadful injury against Liverpool and perhaps a missing yard of pace could possibly have kept him out of a Scotland jersey.

I like to make diagonal runs and I know that John will find me with one of those perfect balls. He never looks as if he is going to hit them hard. He just flights them beautifully and turns defence into attack at one stroke. Football apart, he is one of the best respected people in the game. Nobody has a bad word for him and wherever you go in the football world there is somebody asking about him. He made a miraculous recovery from that Liverpool injury, although it put him out of the game for a year and he suffered another bad one after that. With all his bad luck, there was nobody who deserved the success of Gothenburg more than John – and he made the most of that night. As I say, I just wish he had had more recognition. Nickname: Spammer, from a district known as Spam Valley in his native Greenock.

Neale Cooper is a boy of great potential who has never had the chance to settle in one position. He does an anchor job in midfield but one day he will go back to his natural position of sweeper. He looks like the classical athlete, big and blond, and we tease him about being the good-looking one. He gets all the letters from the girls asking him to marry them. He and his pal, Bryan Gunn, are disco maniacs, into all the tan and gold-chain fashions. But he is a sensible lad just the same and full of boyish good humour, often expressed with impersonations of people like Russ Abbot. Nickname: Tattie (rhyming slang of Neale and tattie-peel).

Alec McLeish is an intelligent big guy and a really good player. He is very mature for his age but we won't see the best of him until he is twenty-seven or twenty-eight, which augurs well for his international career since he is already established in the Scottish team. He made his debut for Scotland in the midfield but is now in his proper position of what used to be called centre half. I used to try and convince him that he was a good passer of a ball though he very seldom took on that role. Now he does a lot of his own passing and has become a much better player as a result. On top of all that, he has a tremendous will to win.

Off the field he is keen on photography, carrying his camera everywhere, occasionally with unfortunate results. At the World Cup, for example, he was snapping away merrily at everybody in sight, including pop star Rod Stewart – only to discover that there wasn't a film in the camera! Nickname: The Westhill Werewolf.

Willie Miller is a truly great player and captain. Having been at the World Cup, I have now played against or watched all the best defenders and I can say, without hesitation, that Willie Miller is the best penalty-box player in the world today. In football, tackling is a fine art which he has perfected to the last move, knowing exactly how to do it and protect himself at the same time. He has such presence in the penalty area that opponents are inclined to be frightened off, as if wondering what they are doing in the same company as this man.

He is the he-man of our Aberdeen team whose concentration has made us all better players. Like a good captain, he speaks up for his players when necessary. Most other times he stays silent, the quiet man of the side who leads by example and only comes out of his shell when he has had a couple of pints. In my naturally perky way, always cracking jokes here and there, I tend to greet the approach of the strong, silent Willie with, 'Here comes John Wayne, lads.' Just as he tackles his opponents, he is busy tackling a bald patch at present, buying a variety of shampoos to stem the attack. Nickname: I call him Millet.

Neil Simpson is the modern midfield player, a hard-working, hard-running lad who defends well, wins tackles in midfield and gets himself into scoring positions as well. His work-rate and general attitude are fairly typical of the Northeast people so it is no coincidence that he is the most truly Northeast player around – a 'loon fae Newmachar' and a real nice loon at that. What's more, he is a growing loon with an appetite that can't even be matched by big Doug and his cream cakes. When he told me he had bought a house I was sure it must be a chip shop with a flat above it. Speaking the Aberdeenshire dialect, he amuses the more ignorant southern players with his phrases. For example, none of us could understand what he meant by 'tummel the cat,' until he put us out of our misery by explaining it meant to somersault. Any Aberdonian would have known it. Nickname: Sunty, which also comes from his Northeast pronunciation of Santa Claus!

Mark McGhee I see more of, away from Pittodrie, than any other player. He is always at my house. But that has nothing to do with my assessment of him as one of the really essential players in the Aberdeen team. He runs well, shoots well and can create goals out of absolutely nothing, which is always the sign of a good player. Aberdeen are the poorer without his strength up front. He can amble into the penalty area and beat one player after another with apparent ease. One observation I would make about Mark is that his instinctive control is better than his conscious control. He is also one of the most intelligent people around Pittodrie (at least, that's what he tells you!). Off the park he reads books that nobody else can understand and is a positive fund of information on things like the nuclear power of Russia compared to America. On a Saturday night Mark and I allow ourselves three pints at a local hotel before joining our wives for the evening. Nickname: Dingus.

John Hewitt, when I first saw him in action, looked likely to be the first million-pound player to leave Scotland. He seemed to have everything – fantastic pace, clever ball control and two great feet. It is one of the ironies of the game that he has been as often on the bench as on the park but what a Super Sub he has turned out to be. His habit of coming on and snatching vital goals was carried right through to the last minutes of Gothenburg. The name of John Hewitt is liable to go down in football history as the man who finally won us the European Cup Winners' Cup and couldn't find a regular place in the team.

There are some valid reasons for his place on the bench, however. With such a gift for acceleration, he doesn't always use it as much as he should. And he has lapses in concentration, which don't exactly please the boss. John speaks very slowly and Fergie will some-times say to him, 'The trouble with you, John, is that you play the way you speak.' But the same lad has time on his side and I hope his career becomes more established, as his talents demand. I have been delighted to see in the 1983–4 season that he has sharpened up his concentration and has therefore been able to command a more regular place in the team. Nickname: Just known as Johnny.

Doug Bell is, in my honest opinion, the best controller of a ball that I have ever seen. And to think that he came to Pittodrie on a free transfer from St Mirren – what a bargain. There is an engine of perpetual motion inside him and his control is such that I don't go near him in training when he has possession. He would just make a fool of me. He would be a Scotland player tomorrow if only he could improve his distribution. He works hard at improvement and I hope he makes the international team. Doug is even more the quiet man of Pittodrie than Willie Miller. He keeps his calm through everything and fears no one. The rumour about his economy with words is that, on his wedding day, when the minister said 'Do you take this woman...' Doug just shrugged his shoul-ders in agreement! Nickname: The Count.

Peter Weir is another former St Mirren player, signed by

Fergie when he was manager at Love Street and the biggest buy that Aberdeen has ever made. The price-tag of around £300,000 weighed heavily on Peter for a time but he need not have worried. He has made a tremendous difference to the Dons, playing wide on the left and sending over a wonderful service of crosses. Fergie spotted, very correctly, that we were lacking a good crosser. Ian Scanlon, who went to St Mirren in part-exchange, was an entertaining runner to the line but he would then turn and twist and you were never sure when his cross would come. Peter is more direct and his percentage of accurate crosses is extremely high. He can cut inside, using both feet to great effect and has a knack of scoring with his head at the back post as well. He was a late developer in the game but has turned into an exciting player, well worth waiting for. Socially, he is another quiet chap, keeping company with his former Love Street team-mate Doug Bell. Nickname: Gas Meter (daft rhyming slang with Peter).

Eric Black led me to make a forecast about his future, when I first saw him. I am even more convinced now that he has the potential to be the best striker in Scotland for the next ten years – a player who will go right to the top, wherever that is. His armoury in striking for goal is phenomenal. He is brilliant on the ground, amazing in the air and has the ability to come away with something new every other week.

He is another of our quiet lads but that will not prevent him becoming a full Scottish internationalist before long. Nickname: Blacko.

Andy Watson has been the first break in the Gothenburg squad, being allowed to leave in the summer of 1983 to join Leeds United. Gaining Under-21 recognition from the Scotland manager, he played a major part in our Premier League Championship win of 1980, coming into the team towards the end of that season and turning things our way with some gritty performances and goals as well. He never did receive the credit he deserved. Not the most skilful of players, he was nevertheless a hard worker who could last to the bitter end. Along with Stuart Kennedy, he has had the best fitness of anyone in my years at Pittodrie. But his career did not progress and he was less in the scheme of things. So he was allowed to go off to Leeds and I have been wondering what Peter Barnes is making of his Aberdeen accent. 'Fit like ma loon' will sound strange to English ears. It took me two years to understand what he was saying. A great lad just the same! Nickname: Winker.

With such a flow of up-and-coming players at Pittodrie, Aberdeen Football Club need never be short of top-class people under its present system, no matter who decides to leave. In the end, the club is always bigger than the individual.

I could pick out lots of promising youngsters but the one nearest to claiming his regular place in the first-team pool at the time of writing is Ian Porteous, though Tom McIntyre has also been showing signs of establishing himself. Both have a lot of promise. I like Porteous's style. He used to be our babysitter and was always ready to talk about football and to confide in us if necessary. Bryan Gunn is a good, big goalkeeper, ready to take his place in most teams but faced with a problem called Jim Leighton. Goalkeepers don't get too many chances to stake their claim and Bryan becomes downhearted at times. There is nothing for it, however, but to plug away until an opportunity arises. Finally, among the playing staff there is a boy called Paul Wright from East Kilbride who is worth keeping an eye on. If my crystal ball is in working order, he is a good professional who will make it to the first team.

Apart from the playing staff, there is one man without whom Pittodrie would be in grave danger of falling down. He is the amazing Teddy Scott, local man and former Dons player of the 1950s, who keeps the place going and attends to everybody's needs. Teddy has a thorough knowledge not only of Aberdeen junior football but the Highland League as well and everyone knows Ted in return. He is particularly good with young players, knows how to talk to them, coax them, push them – a great fellow to have around a club. When I went off to the World Cup in Spain, Teddy had evidently discovered I was suffering from a sore bum. When I arrived and unpacked my belongings, what was tucked away in my bag but a special brand of extra-soft toilet roll! That's Ted.

He is in love with everything to do with the game of football and his loyalty to Aberdeen is complete. He lives out at Ellon, comes chugging in every morning by bus and when he ever gets home I don't know because he always seems to be at Pittodrie. His only break seems to be a game of golf or dominoes on a Sunday. When we started off our European run at Sion in Switzerland, we found we had arrived with the wrong pants. The boss joked that he would have to sack Teddy.

'Where are you going to get the ten people to replace him?' I asked. Everyone knew that wasn't far off the mark.

If Teddy represents a lot of the 'family' side of Aberdeen Football Club then that pattern is set by the chairman himself, Mr Donald, and his fellow directors. I wonder if there is another club where you could expect to find the chairman there at lunchtime, chatting to the players, inquiring about their wives and children and making sure that everybody is happy. If any of us are back training in the afternoon we sometimes take our kids along with us. You are liable to find me playing at goal-kicks with Gavin. The chances are that Mr Donald will be there, always with a fifty-pence piece for the youngsters. Back inside, Teddy will have a bottle of juice for them. That's the family spirit of Aberdeen which is the envy of many another club and which plays its own part in getting things right on the field.

One last word on Mr Donald. He was evidently a great dancer in his younger days and he still walks jauntily through the Pittodrie corridors, whistling a happy tune. Even after defeat he will come whistling into the dressing room to cheer people up. But if he sees the boss's face is tripping him, he has a wonderful way of whistling his way in, walking round the room and whistling his way out again without saying a word!

28

Life at Pittodrie

People often ask me about the daily routine of a footballer, who certainly leads a life that is quite different from any other. The basic week runs from Monday to Friday, forenoons only, with Saturday taking care of itself. I start my day by driving Gavin to school for nine and arriving at Pittodrie by nine-thirty, when I have a cup of tea with Teddy Scott. As the lads arrive individually there is a fair amount of wise-cracking and banter. We discuss what we saw on television last night. There is always the extra interest of waiting to see in which direction Jim Leighton's hair will be standing. With people working so closely together, there has to be a steady undercurrent of humour so we end up behaving like a bunch of wee boys at school.

By nine-thirty the mini-bus is taking the first batch of young lads to Seaton Park, returning for the rest of us. Portable goal posts are erected, practice areas are marked out and we spend the next two hours at training, which varies from day to day so that nothing becomes stale. Dead-ball practice is usually reserved for Wednesday or Friday. At the beginning of the season there is some running exercise but almost everything else we do is geared directly to what will happen on the field of play.

As tacticians, Fergie and Archie have had some great ideas. They would build up moves from one-touch football and so on. We do a lot of 'box work,' in which we practise with two players against five. That has sharpened up Doug Rougvie's game tremendously.

Our routine on home match days is to meet at the Ferryhill Hotel for lunch at noon, which has been especially handy for me with my house in Albury Road. Lesley gets up early and takes the kids out so that I can have some peace on the morning of the game. I usually lie in bed until eleven o'clock. Lunch at the Ferryhill can be fish or chicken or, in my case, just poached eggs on toast. Some players follow that with ice cream and Neil Simpson always has his glass of water. After lunch we go to the lounge to watch *On the Ball* on television and to see what Jimmy Greaves is saying to insult Scottish goal-keepers this week. Then we make our own way to Pittodrie, arriving at one-thirty for the last meeting to run over the plans for the day. There is a final psyching-up time, we collect our pair of complimentary tickets and start getting changed by two o'clock. There is a rub-down with oil – the old linament days are gone for us – then I run out to the park for a warm-up. Meanwhile big Doug is pursuing his own routine in the dressing room, bending, stretching, with arms and legs extending in all directions. For safety's sake, everybody else keeps well out of his way.

Doug and Stuart Kennedy must remember their wee plastic dishes for holding their false teeth. Willie Miller needs his special leg bandage. Then we are ready to take the field as a team, all geared up for the occasion. Alec McLeish insists on being last man out and I like to tie my laces when we reach the pitch. Some chew gum during a game but I have always thought that was a dangerous caper.

When the match is over and the boss has had his say, we find our wives and families in the club lounge where there is a general milling about of people connected with the club in one way or another. The Press can be found in their own hospitality room enjoying a dram and waiting for the two managers to meet them for the usual postmortem. That provides the comments which you read in your Sunday papers next morning. Most players will tell you they can't eat immediately after a game. The chemistry needs to settle and it is some time during the evening before you are ready for a meal.

In any gathering of people you will usually find some who don't pull together. But in my years at Aberdeen there has never been any sign of bad blood between individuals. We all get on together remarkably well. We are not a great lot for socializing with each other but that can be quite a good thing when you are so much in each other's company during the week.

My personal friends tend to be outside football. There's Jim Harper, who works for Shell, and Bill Annal, a local bricklayer, whom I don't see enough of these days with my various commitments. My friend next door at Albury Road, Bob Ralph, is a marine biologist from England who had no interest in football until we met. Now he has a season ticket at Pittodrie.

29

The Fergie Scare

Aberdeen made an erratic start to the 1983–4 season, with some good performances and some very bad ones, until the boss lost his patience and started making noises about the possible break-up of his Gothenburg squad. We were left in no doubt that there would be some of us on the lookout for other clubs if we continued as we were. I believe there was still a hangover from that fabulous season but his warnings seemed to put us back in the right frame of mind. It all came right with an excellent victory over Celtic at Pittodrie and by November we were sitting at the top of the Premier League. As cup winners in Europe we had been expected to make light work of our first opponents in the new competition but Akranes of Iceland gave us more difficulty than we expected.

In the second round of the European Cup Winners' Cup we faced much tougher opposition in the rugged Belgian side, Beveren, but we raised our game against the better team, as so often happens in football. After a goal-less draw in Belgium we were favourites to win at Pittodrie. We didn't anticipate, however, the drama which would take place between those two games.

On the previous Friday, all the speculation which had surrounded the continuing decline of Rangers Football Club boiled over when manager John Greig resigned. For months there had been a lot of talk that Greig might go but what affected us at Pittodrie was the belief that his place would be taken by Alec Ferguson. On that weekend there had been a massive build-up of press opinion that Fergie, the Govan boy and former Rangers player, was all set to manage his old club. Some journalists let their enthusiasm run away with them and James Sanderson was sticking his famous neck so far out on Radio Clyde as to say that Alec Ferguson *would* be in the Ibrox chair by the Monday. He wanted no shilly-shallying, he said, and hoped that Rangers would go straight after their man. Well, well. I'm sure most people in Scotland hoped that he would stay where he was but the pressures on Fergie must have been hard to resist. Aberdeen supporters had a bad few days, dreading not only the loss of their splendid manager but the fact that he would be going to a rival for whom they had no particular liking.

We went to play Dundee at Dens Park that Saturday and quietly tried to gauge what the boss might be thinking. He said absolutely nothing and we were far too professional to let it upset us. As we beat Dundee and turned up at Pittodrie on the Monday morning, the papers were even more certain that it was only a matter of hours before Alec Ferguson signed for Rangers. That lucrative contract on offer from Aberdeen had never actually been signed and people were taking it as a sign that Fergie was holding off in case the Rangers job arose.

We knew there had been a meeting between the manager and the directors but still there was nothing but silence. We were due to meet Beveren at Pittodrie in two days' time. Was he delaying an announcement about going to Rangers until after that match so as not to upset the team? We didn't know. On the Wednesday morning of the match, Willie Miller and I arrived at Pittodrie and passed the boss's door. He just looked at us and said, 'You better get that smile off your faces – I'm here for another five years!'

That was how we knew that he had signed his Aberdeen contract, supposed to be worth about £300,000 for five years, and that Dons supporters everywhere could heave a sigh of relief. It was all over the radio and television bulletins and made big headlines on the front page of the *Evening Express* that night. A Press conference was called at Pittodrie for the early afternoon and the boss announced that, all things considered, he had decided to stay with the club which had given him his greatest moments. He had considered his wife and family, who were happily settled in the city. Personally, I'm sure his admiration for the chairman, Mr Donald, and the board of directors had a lot to do with it. Many people could hardly believe that a Govan man like Fergie had turned down the Ibrox job but most of us in the game were convinced that he had done the right thing. Rangers could solve their own problems, turning next to Jim McLean of Dundee United who gave them a double blow by taking the same attitude as Fergie. The job was finally accepted by Jock Wallace, who was returning to his beloved Ibrox from Motherwell, having started the whole managerial roundabout in 1978 by resigning from the post he was now taking up for the second time.

While a few journalists were wiping the egg off their faces, Aberdeen was gearing itself up for a great night of celebration at Pittodrie. Win or lose against Beveren, the more important news which had spread around the whole country was that Fergie was here to stay. Despite a steady drizzle, every seat in the stadium was filled as we marched out with Beveren for a match which would decide who was to compete in the quarterfinals of the European Cup Winners' Cup in the spring of 1984. The crowd rose to their feet and chanted the name 'Fergie, Fergie'. It was their way of thanking the man who had brought them their greatest moments. Defeat was unthinkable on a night like that. In the first half, John Hewitt made a remarkable run after a long pass from Willie Miller, only to be up-ended by the Beveren goalkeeper. I scored from the penalty spot. Neil Simpson headed a second before half-time and there was never any doubt about the final result. Peter Weir slipped me the perfect pass to score a third and Peter himself, playing a magnificent game, completed our scoring.

Beveren pulled one back but, at 4–1, we were through once again to the last eight of the contest we had won last May.

At that stage of the previous season, we were ready to face Bayern Munich, and people were beginning to wonder if it could happen all over again.

As a follow-up to Gothenburg, we still had to compete for the European Super Cup, an unofficial contest between the winners of the European Cup and the European Cup Winners' Cup to decide once and for all which is the top team in Europe.

Our opponents were to be Hamburg, who had beaten Juventus of Italy in the final of the European Cup, and the first leg in Hamburg ended in a no-scoring draw. So Pittodrie was set for another big night, the first time a major award could actually be presented on our own ground. Hamburg came to Aberdeen amid talk of trouble in the dressing room, but we didn't allow the rumours to distract us.

Out we went that night of 20 December 1983, in a downpour of rain, to find that, in the first half, the Germans were playing some rather attractive possession football. But it lacked bite and at half-time there was no scoring.

Immediately after the interval Peter Weir left Kaltz standing as he raced up the left wing towards the King Street end and crossed an inviting ball. John Hewitt raced in and cut it back for Neil Simpson to put us one up. From a Peter Weir corner on the right, Willie Miller appeared on the left and side-footed the ball across goal for Mark McGhee to make it two.

From then on it was a steady procession towards the German goal and we might have scored five or six. But we had done enough to win the Super Cup, the final icing on the cake, and to convince the doubters that our Cup Winners' Cup victory was no fluke and that we were without question the best team in Europe in 1983.

The future of the club looked good. Fergie was here to stay. I was tempted to stay with success in a place where

I had had many happy years. Yet I knew that I would have regrets if I didn't test my talents in another country.

You must have targets in your career. My first one was to do well in Scotland, remembering that I could have gone to Manchester United as a schoolboy. I then wanted to reach the international team and to do well in Europe. All that had now been achieved. If I am now on my way to another club, I hope my friends in Aberdeen will not hold it against me. Believe me, I love the city and the people of the Northeast and would never want to lose my ties with them. But people in other jobs have their ambitions and we in football have much less time in which to achieve ours. All I want is to make the most of whatever talents I may have. I could fail and wish I had never left the Dons. My family may not settle elsewhere. But it is something I may have to do.

I hope I have made some contribution to the greatest moments in the history of Aberdeen Football Club and that the Dons will go on from strength to strength, proving that they are there to stay at the top of European football. Wherever I am, I know the first result I'll be looking for at a quarter to five on a Saturday night.

Appearances and Goals

In six years at Aberdeen, up to November 1983, Gordon Strachan appeared for the Dons on 302 occasions and scored 90 goals, 42 of them penalties.

Arriving in November, 1977, he had a poor beginning, appearing only 17 times that season and scoring only once.

By 1978–9, that had improved to 52 appearances and six goals. In 1979–80 he played 60 times and scored 16 goals.

With his bad injury in 1980–81, he was back to 39 appearances and 12 goals.

In 1981–2, he played 58 games and scored 22 times.

In 1982–3, the famous Gothenburg year, he played 55 times and scored 23 times.

These totals include everything from European and domestic matches to friendlies.

In those six years, he played in 165 Premier League matches and scored 45 goals, 24 of them penalties.